Mometrix
TEST PREPARATION

Bridge and Tunnel Officer Exam Secrets Study Guide

Dear Future Exam Success Story

First of all, **THANK YOU** for purchasing Mometrix study materials!

Second, congratulations! You are one of the few determined test-takers who are committed to doing whatever it takes to excel on your exam. **You have come to the right place.** We developed these study materials with one goal in mind: to deliver you the information you need in a format that's concise and easy to use.

In addition to optimizing your guide for the content of the test, we've outlined our recommended steps for breaking down the preparation process into small, attainable goals so you can make sure you stay on track.

We've also analyzed the entire test-taking process, identifying the most common pitfalls and showing how you can overcome them and be ready for any curveball the test throws you.

Standardized testing is one of the biggest obstacles on your road to success, which only increases the importance of doing well in the high-pressure, high-stakes environment of test day. Your results on this test could have a significant impact on your future, and this guide provides the information and practical advice to help you achieve your full potential on test day.

Your success is our success

We would love to hear from you! If you would like to share the story of your exam success or if you have any questions or comments in regard to our products, please contact us at **800-673-8175** or **support@mometrix.com**.

Thanks again for your business and we wish you continued success!

Sincerely,
The Mometrix Test Preparation Team

Written and edited by the Mometrix Exam Secrets Test Prep Team
Printed in the United States of America

Table of Contents

Introduction

Thank you for purchasing this resource! You have made the choice to prepare yourself for a test that could have a huge impact on your future, and this guide is designed to help you be fully ready for test day. Obviously, it's important to have a solid understanding of the test material, but you also need to be prepared for the unique environment and stressors of the test, so that you can perform to the best of your abilities.

For this purpose, the first section that appears in this guide is the **Secret Keys**. We've devoted countless hours to meticulously researching what works and what doesn't, and we've boiled down our findings to the five most impactful steps you can take to improve your performance on the test. We start at the beginning with study planning and move through the preparation process, all the way to the testing strategies that will help you get the most out of what you know when you're finally sitting in front of the test.

We recommend that you start preparing for your test as far in advance as possible. However, if you've bought this guide as a last-minute study resource and only have a few days before your test, we recommend that you skip over the first two Secret Keys since they address a long-term study plan.

If you struggle with **test anxiety**, we strongly encourage you to check out our recommendations for how you can overcome it. Test anxiety is a formidable foe, but it can be beaten, and we want to make sure you have the tools you need to defeat it.

Secret Key #1 – Plan Big, Study Small

There's a lot riding on your performance. If you want to ace this test, you're going to need to keep your skills sharp and the material fresh in your mind. You need a plan that lets you review everything you need to know while still fitting in your schedule. We'll break this strategy down into three categories.

Information Organization

Start with the information you already have: the official test outline. From this, you can make a complete list of all the concepts you need to cover before the test. Organize these concepts into groups that can be studied together, and create a list of any related vocabulary you need to learn so you can brush up on any difficult terms. You'll want to keep this vocabulary list handy once you actually start studying since you may need to add to it along the way.

Time Management

Once you have your set of study concepts, decide how to spread them out over the time you have left before the test. Break your study plan into small, clear goals so you have a manageable task for each day and know exactly what you're doing. Then just focus on one small step at a time. When you manage your time this way, you don't need to spend hours at a time studying. Studying a small block of content for a short period each day helps you retain information better and avoid stressing over how much you have left to do. You can relax knowing that you have a plan to cover everything in time. In order for this strategy to be effective though, you have to start studying early and stick to your schedule. Avoid the exhaustion and futility that comes from last-minute cramming!

Study Environment

The environment you study in has a big impact on your learning. Studying in a coffee shop, while probably more enjoyable, is not likely to be as fruitful as studying in a quiet room. It's important to keep distractions to a minimum. You're only planning to study for a short block of time, so make the most of it. Don't pause to check your phone or get up to find a snack. It's also important to **avoid multitasking**. Research has consistently shown that multitasking will make your studying dramatically less effective. Your study area should also be comfortable and well-lit so you don't have the distraction of straining your eyes or sitting on an uncomfortable chair.

The time of day you study is also important. You want to be rested and alert. Don't wait until just before bedtime. Study when you'll be most likely to comprehend and remember. Even better, if you know what time of day your test will be, set that time aside for study. That way your brain will be used to working on that subject at that specific time and you'll have a better chance of recalling information.

Finally, it can be helpful to team up with others who are studying for the same test. Your actual studying should be done in as isolated an environment as possible, but the work of organizing the information and setting up the study plan can be divided up. In between study sessions, you can discuss with your teammates the concepts that you're all studying and quiz each other on the details. Just be sure that your teammates are as serious about the test as you are. If you find that your study time is being replaced with social time, you might need to find a new team.

Secret Key #2 – Make Your Studying Count

You're devoting a lot of time and effort to preparing for this test, so you want to be absolutely certain it will pay off. This means doing more than just reading the content and hoping you can remember it on test day. It's important to make every minute of study count. There are two main areas you can focus on to make your studying count.

Retention

It doesn't matter how much time you study if you can't remember the material. You need to make sure you are retaining the concepts. To check your retention of the information you're learning, try recalling it at later times with minimal prompting. Try carrying around flashcards and glance at one or two from time to time or ask a friend who's also studying for the test to quiz you.

To enhance your retention, look for ways to put the information into practice so that you can apply it rather than simply recalling it. If you're using the information in practical ways, it will be much easier to remember. Similarly, it helps to solidify a concept in your mind if you're not only reading it to yourself but also explaining it to someone else. Ask a friend to let you teach them about a concept you're a little shaky on (or speak aloud to an imaginary audience if necessary). As you try to summarize, define, give examples, and answer your friend's questions, you'll understand the concepts better and they will stay with you longer. Finally, step back for a big picture view and ask yourself how each piece of information fits with the whole subject. When you link the different concepts together and see them working together as a whole, it's easier to remember the individual components.

Finally, practice showing your work on any multi-step problems, even if you're just studying. Writing out each step you take to solve a problem will help solidify the process in your mind, and you'll be more likely to remember it during the test.

Modality

Modality simply refers to the means or method by which you study. Choosing a study modality that fits your own individual learning style is crucial. No two people learn best in exactly the same way, so it's important to know your strengths and use them to your advantage.

For example, if you learn best by visualization, focus on visualizing a concept in your mind and draw an image or a diagram. Try color-coding your notes, illustrating them, or creating symbols that will trigger your mind to recall a learned concept. If you learn best by hearing or discussing information, find a study partner who learns the same way or read aloud to yourself. Think about how to put the information in your own words. Imagine that you are giving a lecture on the topic and record yourself so you can listen to it later.

For any learning style, flashcards can be helpful. Organize the information so you can take advantage of spare moments to review. Underline key words or phrases. Use different colors for different categories. Mnemonic devices (such as creating a short list in which every item starts with the same letter) can also help with retention. Find what works best for you and use it to store the information in your mind most effectively and easily.

Secret Key #3 – Practice the Right Way

Your success on test day depends not only on how many hours you put into preparing, but also on whether you prepared the right way. It's good to check along the way to see if your studying is paying off. One of the most effective ways to do this is by taking practice tests to evaluate your progress. Practice tests are useful because they show exactly where you need to improve. Every time you take a practice test, pay special attention to these three groups of questions:

- The questions you got wrong
- The questions you had to guess on, even if you guessed right
- The questions you found difficult or slow to work through

This will show you exactly what your weak areas are, and where you need to devote more study time. Ask yourself why each of these questions gave you trouble. Was it because you didn't understand the material? Was it because you didn't remember the vocabulary? Do you need more repetitions on this type of question to build speed and confidence? Dig into those questions and figure out how you can strengthen your weak areas as you go back to review the material.

Additionally, many practice tests have a section explaining the answer choices. It can be tempting to read the explanation and think that you now have a good understanding of the concept. However, an explanation likely only covers part of the question's broader context. Even if the explanation makes perfect sense, **go back and investigate** every concept related to the question until you're positive you have a thorough understanding.

As you go along, keep in mind that the practice test is just that: practice. Memorizing these questions and answers will not be very helpful on the actual test because it is unlikely to have any of the same exact questions. If you only know the right answers to the sample questions, you won't be prepared for the real thing. **Study the concepts** until you understand them fully, and then you'll be able to answer any question that shows up on the test.

It's important to wait on the practice tests until you're ready. If you take a test on your first day of study, you may be overwhelmed by the amount of material covered and how much you need to learn. Work up to it gradually.

On test day, you'll need to be prepared for answering questions, managing your time, and using the test-taking strategies you've learned. It's a lot to balance, like a mental marathon that will have a big impact on your future. Like training for a marathon, you'll need to start slowly and work your way up. When test day arrives, you'll be ready.

Start with the strategies you've read in the first two Secret Keys—plan your course and study in the way that works best for you. If you have time, consider using multiple study resources to get different approaches to the same concepts. It can be helpful to see difficult concepts from more than one angle. Then find a good source for practice tests. Many times, the test website will suggest potential study resources or provide sample tests.

Practice Test Strategy

If you're able to find at least three practice tests, we recommend this strategy:

Untimed and Open-Book Practice

Take the first test with no time constraints and with your notes and study guide handy. Take your time and focus on applying the strategies you've learned.

Timed and Open-Book Practice

Take the second practice test open-book as well, but set a timer and practice pacing yourself to finish in time.

Timed and Closed-Book Practice

Take any other practice tests as if it were test day. Set a timer and put away your study materials. Sit at a table or desk in a quiet room, imagine yourself at the testing center, and answer questions as quickly and accurately as possible.

Keep repeating timed and closed-book tests on a regular basis until you run out of practice tests or it's time for the actual test. Your mind will be ready for the schedule and stress of test day, and you'll be able to focus on recalling the material you've learned.

Secret Key #4 – Pace Yourself

Once you're fully prepared for the material on the test, your biggest challenge on test day will be managing your time. Just knowing that the clock is ticking can make you panic even if you have plenty of time left. Work on pacing yourself so you can build confidence against the time constraints of the exam. Pacing is a difficult skill to master, especially in a high-pressure environment, so **practice is vital**.

Set time expectations for your pace based on how much time is available. For example, if a section has 60 questions and the time limit is 30 minutes, you know you have to average 30 seconds or less per question in order to answer them all. Although 30 seconds is the hard limit, set 25 seconds per question as your goal, so you reserve extra time to spend on harder questions. When you budget extra time for the harder questions, you no longer have any reason to stress when those questions take longer to answer.

Don't let this time expectation distract you from working through the test at a calm, steady pace, but keep it in mind so you don't spend too much time on any one question. Recognize that taking extra time on one question you don't understand may keep you from answering two that you do understand later in the test. If your time limit for a question is up and you're still not sure of the answer, mark it and move on, and come back to it later if the time and the test format allow. If the testing format doesn't allow you to return to earlier questions, just make an educated guess; then put it out of your mind and move on.

On the easier questions, be careful not to rush. It may seem wise to hurry through them so you have more time for the challenging ones, but it's not worth missing one if you know the concept and just didn't take the time to read the question fully. Work efficiently but make sure you understand the question and have looked at all of the answer choices, since more than one may seem right at first.

Even if you're paying attention to the time, you may find yourself a little behind at some point. You should speed up to get back on track, but do so wisely. Don't panic; just take a few seconds less on each question until you're caught up. Don't guess without thinking, but do look through the answer choices and eliminate any you know are wrong. If you can get down to two choices, it is often worthwhile to guess from those. Once you've chosen an answer, move on and don't dwell on any that you skipped or had to hurry through. If a question was taking too long, chances are it was one of the harder ones, so you weren't as likely to get it right anyway.

On the other hand, if you find yourself getting ahead of schedule, it may be beneficial to slow down a little. The more quickly you work, the more likely you are to make a careless mistake that will affect your score. You've budgeted time for each question, so don't be afraid to spend that time. Practice an efficient but careful pace to get the most out of the time you have.

Secret Key #5 – Have a Plan for Guessing

When you're taking the test, you may find yourself stuck on a question. Some of the answer choices seem better than others, but you don't see the one answer choice that is obviously correct. What do you do?

The scenario described above is very common, yet most test takers have not effectively prepared for it. Developing and practicing a plan for guessing may be one of the single most effective uses of your time as you get ready for the exam.

In developing your plan for guessing, there are three questions to address:

- When should you start the guessing process?
- How should you narrow down the choices?
- Which answer should you choose?

When to Start the Guessing Process

Unless your plan for guessing is to select C every time (which, despite its merits, is not what we recommend), you need to leave yourself enough time to apply your answer elimination strategies. Since you have a limited amount of time for each question, that means that if you're going to give yourself the best shot at guessing correctly, you have to decide quickly whether or not you will guess.

Of course, the best-case scenario is that you don't have to guess at all, so first, see if you can answer the question based on your knowledge of the subject and basic reasoning skills. Focus on the key words in the question and try to jog your memory of related topics. Give yourself a chance to bring the knowledge to mind, but once you realize that you don't have (or you can't access) the knowledge you need to answer the question, it's time to start the guessing process.

It's almost always better to start the guessing process too early than too late. It only takes a few seconds to remember something and answer the question from knowledge. Carefully eliminating wrong answer choices takes longer. Plus, going through the process of eliminating answer choices can actually help jog your memory.

Summary: Start the guessing process as soon as you decide that you can't answer the question based on your knowledge.

How to Narrow Down the Choices

The next chapter in this book (**Test-Taking Strategies**) includes a wide range of strategies for how to approach questions and how to look for answer choices to eliminate. You will definitely want to read those carefully, practice them, and figure out which ones work best for you. Here though, we're going to address a mindset rather than a particular strategy.

Your odds of guessing an answer correctly depend on how many options you are choosing from.

Number of options left	5	4	3	2	1
Odds of guessing correctly	20%	25%	33%	50%	100%

You can see from this chart just how valuable it is to be able to eliminate incorrect answers and make an educated guess, but there are two things that many test takers do that cause them to miss out on the benefits of guessing:

- Accidentally eliminating the correct answer
- Selecting an answer based on an impression

We'll look at the first one here, and the second one in the next section.

To avoid accidentally eliminating the correct answer, we recommend a thought exercise called **the $5 challenge**. In this challenge, you only eliminate an answer choice from contention if you are willing to bet $5 on it being wrong. Why $5? Five dollars is a small but not insignificant amount of money. It's an amount you could afford to lose but wouldn't want to throw away. And while losing $5 once might not hurt too much, doing it twenty times will set you back $100. In the same way, each small decision you make—eliminating a choice here, guessing on a question there—won't by itself impact your score very much, but when you put them all together, they can make a big difference. By holding each answer choice elimination decision to a higher standard, you can reduce the risk of accidentally eliminating the correct answer.

The $5 challenge can also be applied in a positive sense: If you are willing to bet $5 that an answer choice *is* correct, go ahead and mark it as correct.

Summary: Only eliminate an answer choice if you are willing to bet $5 that it is wrong.

Which Answer to Choose

You're taking the test. You've run into a hard question and decided you'll have to guess. You've eliminated all the answer choices you're willing to bet $5 on. Now you have to pick an answer. Why do we even need to talk about this? Why can't you just pick whichever one you feel like when the time comes?

The answer to these questions is that if you don't come into the test with a plan, you'll rely on your impression to select an answer choice, and if you do that, you risk falling into a trap. The test writers know that everyone who takes their test will be guessing on some of the questions, so they intentionally write wrong answer choices to seem plausible. You still have to pick an answer though, and if the wrong answer choices are designed to look right, how can you ever be sure that you're not falling for their trap? The best solution we've found to this dilemma is to take the decision out of your hands entirely. Here is the process we recommend:

Once you've eliminated any choices that you are confident (willing to bet $5) are wrong, select the first remaining choice as your answer.

Whether you choose to select the first remaining choice, the second, or the last, the important thing is that you use some preselected standard. Using this approach guarantees that you will not be enticed into selecting an answer choice that looks right, because you are not basing your decision on how the answer choices look.

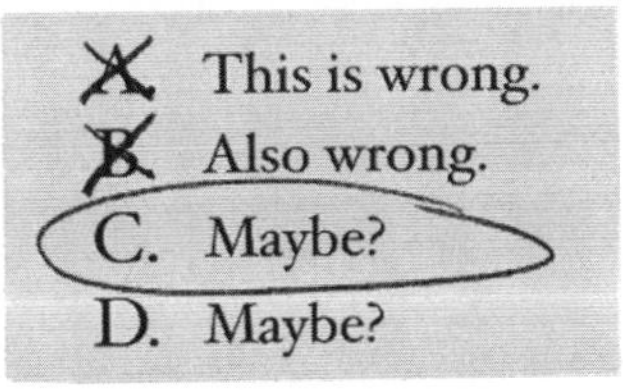

This is not meant to make you question your knowledge. Instead, it is to help you recognize the difference between your knowledge and your impressions. There's a huge difference between thinking an answer is right because of what you know, and thinking an answer is right because it looks or sounds like it should be right.

Summary: To ensure that your selection is appropriately random, make a predetermined selection from among all answer choices you have not eliminated.

Test-Taking Strategies

This section contains a list of test-taking strategies that you may find helpful as you work through the test. By taking what you know and applying logical thought, you can maximize your chances of answering any question correctly!

It is very important to realize that every question is different and every person is different: no single strategy will work on every question, and no single strategy will work for every person. That's why we've included all of them here, so you can try them out and determine which ones work best for different types of questions and which ones work best for you.

Question Strategies

✓ Read Carefully

Read the question and the answer choices carefully. Don't miss the question because you misread the terms. You have plenty of time to read each question thoroughly and make sure you understand what is being asked. Yet a happy medium must be attained, so don't waste too much time. You must read carefully and efficiently.

✓ Contextual Clues

Look for contextual clues. If the question includes a word you are not familiar with, look at the immediate context for some indication of what the word might mean. Contextual clues can often give you all the information you need to decipher the meaning of an unfamiliar word. Even if you can't determine the meaning, you may be able to narrow down the possibilities enough to make a solid guess at the answer to the question.

✓ Prefixes

If you're having trouble with a word in the question or answer choices, try dissecting it. Take advantage of every clue that the word might include. Prefixes can be a huge help. Usually, they allow you to determine a basic meaning. *Pre-* means before, *post-* means after, *pro-* is positive, *de-* is negative. From prefixes, you can get an idea of the general meaning of the word and try to put it into context.

✓ Hedge Words

Watch out for critical hedge words, such as *likely, may, can, often, almost, mostly, usually, generally, rarely,* and *sometimes.* Question writers insert these hedge phrases to cover every possibility. Often an answer choice will be wrong simply because it leaves no room for exception. Be on guard for answer choices that have definitive words such as *exactly* and *always.*

✓ Switchback Words

Stay alert for *switchbacks.* These are the words and phrases frequently used to alert you to shifts in thought. The most common switchback words are *but, although,* and *however.* Others include *nevertheless, on the other hand, even though, while, in spite of, despite,* and *regardless of.* Switchback words are important to catch because they can change the direction of the question or an answer choice.

☑ FACE VALUE

When in doubt, use common sense. Accept the situation in the problem at face value. Don't read too much into it. These problems will not require you to make wild assumptions. If you have to go beyond creativity and warp time or space in order to have an answer choice fit the question, then you should move on and consider the other answer choices. These are normal problems rooted in reality. The applicable relationship or explanation may not be readily apparent, but it is there for you to figure out. Use your common sense to interpret anything that isn't clear.

Answer Choice Strategies

☑ ANSWER SELECTION

The most thorough way to pick an answer choice is to identify and eliminate wrong answers until only one is left, then confirm it is the correct answer. Sometimes an answer choice may immediately seem right, but be careful. The test writers will usually put more than one reasonable answer choice on each question, so take a second to read all of them and make sure that the other choices are not equally obvious. As long as you have time left, it is better to read every answer choice than to pick the first one that looks right without checking the others.

☑ ANSWER CHOICE FAMILIES

An answer choice family consists of two (in rare cases, three) answer choices that are very similar in construction and cannot all be true at the same time. If you see two answer choices that are direct opposites or parallels, one of them is usually the correct answer. For instance, if one answer choice says that quantity *x* increases and another either says that quantity *x* decreases (opposite) or says that quantity *y* increases (parallel), then those answer choices would fall into the same family. An answer choice that doesn't match the construction of the answer choice family is more likely to be incorrect. Most questions will not have answer choice families, but when they do appear, you should be prepared to recognize them.

☑ ELIMINATE ANSWERS

Eliminate answer choices as soon as you realize they are wrong, but make sure you consider all possibilities. If you are eliminating answer choices and realize that the last one you are left with is also wrong, don't panic. Start over and consider each choice again. There may be something you missed the first time that you will realize on the second pass.

☑ AVOID FACT TRAPS

Don't be distracted by an answer choice that is factually true but doesn't answer the question. You are looking for the choice that answers the question. Stay focused on what the question is asking for so you don't accidentally pick an answer that is true but incorrect. Always go back to the question and make sure the answer choice you've selected actually answers the question and is not merely a true statement.

☑ EXTREME STATEMENTS

In general, you should avoid answers that put forth extreme actions as standard practice or proclaim controversial ideas as established fact. An answer choice that states the "process should be used in certain situations, if..." is much more likely to be correct than one that states the "process should be discontinued completely." The first is a calm rational statement and doesn't even make a definitive, uncompromising stance, using a hedge word *if* to provide wiggle room, whereas the second choice is far more extreme.

BENCHMARK

As you read through the answer choices and you come across one that seems to answer the question well, mentally select that answer choice. This is not your final answer, but it's the one that will help you evaluate the other answer choices. The one that you selected is your benchmark or standard for judging each of the other answer choices. Every other answer choice must be compared to your benchmark. That choice is correct until proven otherwise by another answer choice beating it. If you find a better answer, then that one becomes your new benchmark. Once you've decided that no other choice answers the question as well as your benchmark, you have your final answer.

PREDICT THE ANSWER

Before you even start looking at the answer choices, it is often best to try to predict the answer. When you come up with the answer on your own, it is easier to avoid distractions and traps because you will know exactly what to look for. The right answer choice is unlikely to be word-for-word what you came up with, but it should be a close match. Even if you are confident that you have the right answer, you should still take the time to read each option before moving on.

General Strategies

TOUGH QUESTIONS

If you are stumped on a problem or it appears too hard or too difficult, don't waste time. Move on! Remember though, if you can quickly check for obviously incorrect answer choices, your chances of guessing correctly are greatly improved. Before you completely give up, at least try to knock out a couple of possible answers. Eliminate what you can and then guess at the remaining answer choices before moving on.

CHECK YOUR WORK

Since you will probably not know every term listed and the answer to every question, it is important that you get credit for the ones that you do know. Don't miss any questions through careless mistakes. If at all possible, try to take a second to look back over your answer selection and make sure you've selected the correct answer choice and haven't made a costly careless mistake (such as marking an answer choice that you didn't mean to mark). This quick double check should more than pay for itself in caught mistakes for the time it costs.

PACE YOURSELF

It's easy to be overwhelmed when you're looking at a page full of questions; your mind is confused and full of random thoughts, and the clock is ticking down faster than you would like. Calm down and maintain the pace that you have set for yourself. Especially as you get down to the last few minutes of the test, don't let the small numbers on the clock make you panic. As long as you are on track by monitoring your pace, you are guaranteed to have time for each question.

DON'T RUSH

It is very easy to make errors when you are in a hurry. Maintaining a fast pace in answering questions is pointless if it makes you miss questions that you would have gotten right otherwise. Test writers like to include distracting information and wrong answers that seem right. Taking a little extra time to avoid careless mistakes can make all the difference in your test score. Find a pace that allows you to be confident in the answers that you select.

⊘ Keep Moving

Panicking will not help you pass the test, so do your best to stay calm and keep moving. Taking deep breaths and going through the answer elimination steps you practiced can help to break through a stress barrier and keep your pace.

Final Notes

The combination of a solid foundation of content knowledge and the confidence that comes from practicing your plan for applying that knowledge is the key to maximizing your performance on test day. As your foundation of content knowledge is built up and strengthened, you'll find that the strategies included in this chapter become more and more effective in helping you quickly sift through the distractions and traps of the test to isolate the correct answer.

Now that you're preparing to move forward into the test content chapters of this book, be sure to keep your goal in mind. As you read, think about how you will be able to apply this information on the test. If you've already seen sample questions for the test and you have an idea of the question format and style, try to come up with questions of your own that you can answer based on what you're reading. This will give you valuable practice applying your knowledge in the same ways you can expect to on test day.

Good luck and good studying!

Written Comprehension

What Are These Questions Testing?

Written Comprehension questions are measuring your ability to quickly grasp and retain important information in written passages.

The ability to quickly and accurately comprehend information expressed in a written form is critical to success in any career.

What Is the Question Format?

The questions in Written Comprehension will share a similar format. You'll be given a reading passage which is usually about one paragraph long. In most cases, there will be a lot going on in the passage. It may describe several different events or feature a single event with several different people and/or items involved. Following the passage, one or more questions about it will be shown. In each one, you'll be asked about something you read in the passage. It will usually be some detail about a person or action described in the passage. In other words, after you read each question, you'll usually need to go back and dig through the passage to find the correct specifics for the answer.

What Strategies or Techniques Can I Use to Do Well on This Section?

In the Written Comprehension section, you'll need to balance two things—speed and accuracy. Ideally, you would be able to go at your own pace, and read as slowly as you need to in order to make sure your accuracy is perfect. However, you'll be up against a time limit, which means you can't necessarily take as much time as you'd like and read at a nice, leisurely pace. In other words, you have a dilemma—if you go too fast, you risk making errors, but if you go too slowly, you risk not answering all the questions. However, the test is designed so that the average person should have no trouble reading fast enough to answer all the questions, without sacrificing accuracy. Although it may sound trite, the key to success is to not worry about your speed when reading the passage. You should read at about the same pace you use in everyday reading.

Unless you have a lot of difficulty reading, answering these questions isn't complicated. The questions are pretty straightforward—who did what, where did an action take place, how many suspects were there, etc. However, the main reason people do poorly on this section is because there's usually quite a bit of information in each passage, and it's very easy to confuse one person or item or location for another and select the wrong answer. To avoid this, a very effective strategy you can use is to read the questions before reading the actual passage, so you know what you're looking for. Of course, you should also make certain you've read each question very carefully. If necessary and if you have time, read each question at least twice—once before you look for the answer in the passage, and again after you've selected an answer choice. For most people, the two steps of reading the questions before reading the passage, and then reading the question again after an answer has been chosen, are probably the best ways to of improving their chances of making a good score in Written Comprehension.

It is also important to practice ahead of time. This guide has many questions you can use for practice, but you don't need to stop there. Pick up a book or a magazine and read a brief passage from it that contains a lot of details. Then give the reading material to a friend or family member and have them quiz you over it to see how many details you can recall correctly. Do this on a regular basis and you'll be far better prepared for these questions than the average person taking the test. In addition, the peace of mind you'll have knowing that you're prepared will help you stay relaxed and focused on the test.

Practice Questions

1. At approximately 2:27 p.m. on Friday, Officer Naomi Jensen and Officer Kurt Sweitzer pulled over a 1992 Jeep Wrangler for a missing tail light. The female driver, who identified herself as Cindy Ortega, and the male passenger, who said his name was Jesse Ruiz, appeared to both officers to be acting in a suspicious manner, and neither one had any form of identification with them. The driver gave permission for a search of the vehicle, and in the trunk officers discovered two purse and two wallets which appeared to be stolen from elderly people, and several expensive items which had recently been purchased, still in their bags. On questioning, Cindy Ortega admitted that the items had been purchased with stolen credit cards taken from the wallets and purses, which they had obtained from an associate who works in a nursing home.

Why did the officers pull the car over originally?

a. Missing tail light
b. Running a stop sign
c. Failure to yield
d. Speeding in a school zone

2. At 9:12 on the evening of July 23rd, officers of the West Side 2nd Division were dispatched to the 4400 block of Gina Dr to investigate a call about a reported domestic disturbance involving a gun. Officers Thelma Swihart and Vernon Fournier arrived at the scene and determined that there was a disturbance between the occupants of an apartment and several parties who showed up at the residence, and that the disturbance stemmed from a child custody dispute. Questioning revealed that the seven parties who showed up at the apartment illegally entered it, assaulting the occupants in the process, and threatened them with further harm, kidnapping, and death. The male occupant retrieved a handgun to defend himself but several of the suspects managed to wrest it from him. No shots were fired during the disturbance. The seven suspects who showed up at the residence were arrested for multiple charges including 1st Degree Burglary, Assault, Harassment, Battery, and Child Abuse. All seven parties were later booked into the El Paso County Criminal Justice Center on those charges.

How many officers were at the scene?

a. Two
b. Three
c. Four
d. Five

3. In early November, the police department began receiving calls about a man passing counterfeit currency at stores. On November 4, a pizza restaurant called the police and said that after closing they noticed that one of the $20 bills in the cash register looked funny. Officers determined that it was indeed a counterfeit bill. The store manager said no one there remembered who they got it from. The next day, police were called to a mobile phone store downtown, where the manager turned over twenty $20 bills a man had attempted to pay for a phone with. When the manager began scrutinizing the bills, the man fled the store. Officers got a good description of the man from the store personnel. On November 8, the same thing happened at another phone store, where a man matching the description fled the store after trying to pass $300 in phony $20 bills. On November 9, the man was finally captured when an off-duty officer happened to be in a jewelry store when the man tried to purchase a $2000 ring with counterfeit bills. When the store manager became suspicious, the man started to flee, but the off-duty officer was able to restrain him. A few minutes later, two officers arrived and arrested him on counterfeiting charges.

On which day did the man try to pass $400 in fake currency at a phone store?

a. November 4
b. November 5
c. November 6
d. November 8

4. On Sunday, May 18, approximately 17:19, two members of the police department responded to the vicinity of I-10 and 11th Avenue regarding a call from a motorist about shots being fired. Initial information provided by the caller indicated that an unknown suspect was shooting at cars while traveling on the interstate and that one of the bullets struck her back window. The caller advised that her husband and child were also in the vehicle with her. The caller said she could not provide any information about the suspect, or any reason anyone would want to shoot her. Officers were able to locate the caller's vehicle at the intersection of 11th Avenue and Gladys Street. The officers were able to verify that the rear window appeared to be shot out. The officers attempted to pull the car over but the driver, who turned out to be the husband of the caller, refused to pull over and a brief pursuit ensued. Officers were able to make contact with the occupants of the caller's vehicle when the driver finally pulled over at the intersection of 11th Avenue and College Street. During further investigation the officers learned that the callers, Heather Bates, was also the suspect, as she had actually fired several shots inside the vehicle in close proximity to her toddler child. The story that someone else had been shooting at the car turned out to be false. Heather Bates was booked into the Jefferson County Justice Center on the charges of Possession of a Weapon by a Previous Offender, Child Abuse, and Reckless Endangerment. Her husband, Steve Bates, was cited and released for Misdemeanor Vehicular Eluding and Child Abuse.

Where was the caller's car pulled over?

a. I-10 and 11th Avenue
b. I-10 and Gladys Street
c. Gladys Street and College Street
d. 11th Avenue and College Street

5. On May 2, at approximately 2:05 a.m., a caller reported there had been a road rage incident. The caller said the suspect pickup truck rammed the victim's car at the intersection of Calder Avenue and 8th Street, and then a male passenger in the truck had pointed a gun at the victim before fleeing the scene. As officers were on the way to the area, another call was received from a few blocks away, near the intersection of Calder Avenue and MLK Parkway. The caller stated that a pickup truck matching the suspect vehicle description was stopped in the middle of the street and several males had gotten out of the truck and were kicking it and smashing it with rocks. They then fled the area on foot and were not located. Officers determined that the truck from the road rage incident was a stolen vehicle that had not been reported stolen yet. It turned out that it had been stolen from a residence near the intersection of 9th Street and Hazel Avenue. The truck also contained property that had been stolen out of a different vehicle at a residence near the intersection of Ashley Avenue and 10th Street. No arrests have been made at this time; police describe the suspects as four white or Hispanic males in their early 20s.

The personal property was taken from a vehicle near the intersection of:

a. Calder Avenue and MLK Parkway
b. Calder Avenue and 8th Street
c. Ashley Avenue and 10th Street
d. 9th Street and Hazel Avenue

Practice Answers

1. A: Missing tail light. This is stated in the first sentence of the passage.

2. A: Two. Officers Thelma Swihart and Vernon Fournier were at the scene.

3. B: November 5. On the day after November 4, the suspect tried to pay for a phone with $400 worth of phony $20 bills.

4. D: 11th Avenue and College Street. Officers were able to make contact with the occupants of the caller's vehicle when the driver finally pulled over at the intersection of 11th Avenue and College Street.

5. C: Ashley Avenue and 10th Street. Calder and MLK is where the suspects were kicking and throwing rocks at the truck. Calder and 8th Street was the scene of the hit and run the truck was involved in. The truck had been stolen from a residence near the intersection of 9th Street and Hazel Avenue. The truck contained property that had been stolen out of a different vehicle at a residence near the intersection of Ashley Avenue and 10th Street.

Written Expression

The Written Expression section measures your language abilities. On this part of the exam, you'll be tested for your ability to express your thoughts to others in the written language, while using proper grammar and spelling. In your job, you will be expected to speak and write in a way that demonstrates professionalism when dealing with the public, co-workers, superiors, etc.

What Is the Question Format?

The format of the questions in Written Expression is simple and straightforward. There are two kinds—spelling and grammar. In questions about spelling, you'll be shown a sentence in which one of the words has been spelled incorrectly. In the answer choices, you'll be shown four of the words from the sentence, three of which are spelled correctly, and you'll have to choose the one that is misspelled. In the second type of question, you'll be given a sentence with a blank representing a missing word. You'll be asked to choose which of the four answer choices should go in the blank.

What Strategies or Techniques Can I Use to Do Well on This Section?

There are two things you can do that will really help you improve your potential score in this section. First, if you don't read on a regular basis, you should start doing so immediately, and do a little reading every day between now and when you take the test. It's almost impossible to memorize all the rules of grammar and spelling. We learn grammar primarily from exposure on a daily basis. However, most people don't use proper grammar when they speak, as the spoken word is much more casual than most written text. Of course, when it comes to spelling, the spoken word isn't much help. Thus, it's important to read a little bit every day.

Newspaper and magazine articles, either in print on online, are great for easy exposure. These kinds of publications use trained, professional writers and expect them to use proper grammar and correct spelling. They also have several editors inspecting each writer's text for mistakes in spelling and grammar before they publish. Reading this kind of material every day will increase your ability to tell the difference between good and poor grammar.

The second thing you can do is review this chapter every day. In it, you'll find an easy to read, but pretty thorough, guide to grammar and spelling, covering the main things you'll need to know. You'll learn the main rules of spelling, as well as the exceptions to those rules. We also show you the main components of good grammar, explain their purpose, and give you the rules for using good grammar. This will allow you to understand why something is either right or wrong. None of it is very complicated, and there's no reason you can't master it. The key is to study and review a little bit each day. As you do so, your skills and your confidence in your abilities will steadily increase, and you'll be ready for the Written Expression section when test day arrives.

Grammar

Subject-Verb Agreement

Verbs must agree with their subjects in number. In other words, singular subjects need singular verbs. Plural subjects need plural verbs. Singular is for one person, place, or thing. Plural is for more than one person, place, or thing. Subjects and verbs must also agree in person: first, second, or third. The present tense ending *-s* is used on a verb if its subject is third person singular; otherwise, the verb takes no ending.

Review Video: Subject-Verb Agreement
Visit mometrix.com/academy and enter code: 479190

Number Agreement Examples

Single Subject and Verb: *Dan calls home.*

(Dan is one person. So, the singular verb *calls* is needed.)

Plural Subject and Verb: *Dan and Bob call home.*

(More than one person needs the plural verb *call.*)

Person Agreement Examples

First Person: I *am* walking.

Second Person: You *are* walking.

Third Person: He *is* walking.

Problems with Subject-Verb Agreement

Words between Subject and Verb

The joy of my life returns home tonight.

(**Singular Subject**: joy. **Singular Verb**: returns)

The phrase *of my life* does not influence the verb *returns.*

The question that still remains unanswered is "Who are you?"

(**Singular Subject**: question. **Singular Verb**: is)

Don't let the phrase "*that still remains…*" trouble you. The subject *questions* goes with *is.*

Compound Subjects

You and Jon are invited to come to my house.

(**Plural Subject**: You and Jon. **Plural Verb**: are)

The pencil and paper belong to me.

(**Plural Subject**: pencil and paper. **Plural Verb**: belong)

Subjects Joined by Or and Nor

Today or tomorrow is the day.

(**Subject**: Today / tomorrow. **Verb**: is)

Stan or Phil wants to read the book.

(**Subject**: Stan / Phil. **Verb**: wants)

Neither the books nor the *pen is* on the desk.

(**Subject**: Books / Pen. **Verb**: was)

Either the blanket or *pillows arrive* this afternoon.

(**Subject**: Blanket / Pillows. **Verb**: arrive)

Note: Singular subjects that are joined with the conjunction *or* need a singular verb. However, when one subject is singular and another is plural, you make the verb agree with the closer subject. The example about books and the pen has a singular verb because the pen (singular subject) is closer to the verb.

Indefinite Pronouns: Either, Neither, and Each

Is either of you ready for the game?

(**Singular Subject**: Either. **Singular Verb**: is)

Each man, woman, and child is unique.

(**Singular Subject**: Each. **Singular Verb**: is)

The Adjective Every and Compounds: Everybody, Everyone, Anybody, Anyone

Every day passes faster than the last.

(**Singular Subject**: Every day. **Singular Verb**: passes)

Anybody is welcome to bring a tent.

(**Singular Subject**: Anybody. **Singular Verb**: is)

Collective Nouns

The family eats at the restaurant every Friday night.

(The members of the family are one at the restaurant.)

The team are leaving for their homes after the game.

(The members of the team are leaving as individuals to go to their own homes.)

Who, Which, and That as Subject

This is the man who is helping me today.

He is a good man who serves others before himself.

This painting that is hung over the couch is very beautiful.

Plural Form and Singular Meaning

Some nouns that are singular in meaning but plural in form: news, mathematics, physics, and economics

The news is coming on now.

Mathematics is my favorite class.

Some nouns that are plural in meaning: athletics, gymnastics, scissors, and pants

Do these pants come with a shirt?

The scissors are for my project.

Note: There are more nouns in plural form and are singular in meaning than plural in meaning. Look to your dictionary for help when you don't know about the meaning of a verb.

Addition, Multiplication, Subtraction, and Division are normally singular.

One plus one is two.

Three times three is nine.

COMPLEMENTS

A complement is a noun, pronoun, or adjective that is used to give more information about the verb in the sentence.

DIRECT OBJECTS

A direct object is a noun that takes or receives the action of a verb. Remember: a complete sentence does not need a direct object. A sentence needs only a subject and a verb. When you are looking for a direct object, find the verb and ask *who* or *what.*

Example: I took the blanket. (Who or what did I take? *The blanket*)

Jane read books. (Who or what does Jane read? *Books*)

INDIRECT OBJECTS

An indirect object is a word or group of words that show how an action had an influence on someone or something. If there is an indirect object in a sentence, then you always have a direct object in the sentence. When you are looking for the indirect object, find the verb and ask *to/for whom or what.*

Examples: We taught the old dog a new trick.

(To/For Whom or What was taught? *The old dog*)

I gave them a math lesson.

(To/For Whom or What was given? *Them*)

Review Video: Direct and Indirect Objects
Visit mometrix.com/academy and enter code: 817385

Predicate Nouns are nouns that modify the subject and finish linking verbs.

Example: My father is a lawyer.

Father is the subject. Lawyer is the predicate noun.

Predicate Adjectives are adjectives that modify the subject and finish linking verbs.

Example: Your mother is patient.

Mother is the subject. Patient is the predicate adjective.

Pronoun Usage

Pronoun-antecedent agreement – The antecedent is the noun that has been replaced by a pronoun. A pronoun and the antecedent agree when they are singular or plural.

Singular agreement: *John* came into town, and *he* played for us.

(The word *He* replaces *John*.)

Plural agreement: *John and Rick* came into town, and *they* played for us.

(The word *They* replaces *John* and *Rick*.)

To know the correct pronoun for a compound subject, try each pronoun separately with the verb. Your knowledge of pronouns will tell you which one is correct.

Example: Bob and (I, me) will be going.

(Answer: Bob and I will be going.)

(1) *I will be going* or (2) *Me will be going*. The second choice cannot be correct because *me* is not used as a subject of a sentence. Instead, *me* is used as an object.

When a pronoun is used with a noun immediately following (as in "we boys"), try the sentence without the added noun.

Example: (We/Us) boys played football last year.

(Answer: We boys played football last year.)

(1) *We* played football last year or (2) *Us* played football last year. Again, the second choice cannot be correct because *us* is not used as a subject of a sentence. Instead, *us* is used as an object.

Review Video: Pronoun Usage
Visit mometrix.com/academy and enter code: 666500

Pronoun reference – A pronoun should point clearly to the antecedent. Here is how a pronoun reference can be unhelpful if it is not directly stated or puzzling.

Unhelpful: Ron and Jim went to the store, and he bought soda.

(Who bought soda? Ron or Jim?)

Helpful: Jim went to the store, and he bought soda.

(The sentence is clear. Jim bought the soda.)

Personal pronouns – Some pronouns change their form by their placement in a sentence. A pronoun that is a subject in a sentence comes in the subjective case. Pronouns that serve as objects appear in the objective case. Finally, the pronouns that are used as possessives appear in the possessive case.

Subjective case: *He* is coming to the show.

(The pronoun *He* is the subject of the sentence.)

Objective case: Josh drove *him* to the airport.

(The pronoun *him* is the object of the sentence.)

Possessive case: The flowers are *mine*.

(The pronoun *mine* shows ownership of the flowers.)

Who or whom – *Who*, a subjective-case pronoun, can be used as a subject. *Whom*, an objective case pronoun, can be used as an object. The words *who* and *whom* are common in subordinate clauses or in questions.

Subject: He knows who wants to come.

(*Who* is the subject of the verb *wants*.)

Object: He knows whom we want at the party.

(*Whom* is the object of *we want*.)

Sentence Structures

The four major types of sentence structure are:

1. Simple Sentences – Simple sentences have one independent clause with no subordinate clauses. A simple sentence can have compound elements (e.g., a compound subject or verb).

   Examples:

   Judy watered the lawn. (Singular Subject & Singular Predicate)
   Judy and Alan watered the lawn. (Compound Subject: Judy and Alan)

2. Compound Sentences – Compound sentences have two or more independent clauses with no dependent clauses. Usually, the independent clauses are joined with a comma and a coordinating conjunction, or they can be joined with a semicolon.

   Example:

   The time has come, and we are ready.
   I woke up at dawn; then I went outside to watch the sun rise.

3. Complex Sentences – A complex sentence has one independent clause and one or more dependent clauses.

   Examples:

   Although he had the flu, Harry went to work.
   Marcia got married after she finished college.

4. Compound-Complex Sentences – A compound-complex sentence has at least two independent clauses and at least one dependent clause.

   Examples:

John is my friend who went to India, and he brought souvenirs for us.
You may not know, but we heard the music that you played last night.

Review Video: Sentence Structure
Visit mometrix.com/academy and enter code: 700478

Sentence Fragments

A part of a sentence should not be treated like a complete sentence. A sentence must be made of at least one independent clause. An independent clause has a subject and a verb. Remember that the independent clause can stand alone as a sentence. Some fragments are independent clauses that begin with a subordinating word (e.g., as, because, so, etc.). Other fragments may not have a subject, a verb, or both.

A sentence fragment can be repaired in several ways. One way is to put the fragment with a neighbor sentence. Another way is to be sure that punctuation is not needed. You can also turn the fragment into a sentence by adding any missing pieces. Sentence fragments are allowed for writers who want to show off their art. However, for your exam, sentence fragments are not allowed.

Fragment: Because he wanted to sail for Rome.

Correct: He dreamed of Europe because he wanted to sail for Rome.

Dangling and Misplaced Modifiers

Dangling Modifiers

A dangling modifier is a verbal phrase that does not have a clear connection to a word. A dangling modifier can also be a dependent clause (the subject and/or verb are not included) that does not have a clear connection to a word.

Examples:

Dangling: *Reading each magazine article*, the stories caught my attention.

Corrected: Reading each magazine article, *I* was entertained by the stories.

In this example, the word *stories* cannot be modified by *Reading each magazine article*. People can read, but stories cannot read. So, the pronoun *I* is needed for the modifying phrase *Reading each magazine article*.

Dangling: Since childhood, my grandparents have visited me for Christmas.

Corrected: Since childhood, I have been visited by my grandparents for Christmas.

In this example, the dependent adverb clause *Since childhood* cannot modify grandparents. So, the pronoun *I* is needed for the modifying adverb clause.

Misplaced Modifiers

In some sentences, a modifier can be put in more than one place. However, you need to be sure that there is no confusion about which word is being explained or given more detail.

Incorrect: He read the book to a crowd that was filled with beautiful pictures.

Correct: He read the book that was filled with beautiful pictures to a crowd.

The crowd is not filled with pictures. The book is filled with pictures.

Incorrect: John only ate fruits and vegetables for two weeks.

Correct: John ate *only* fruits and vegetables for two weeks.

John may have done nothing else for two weeks but eat fruits and vegetables and sleep. However, it is reasonable to think that John had fruits and vegetables for his meals. Then, he continued to work on other things.

Run-on Sentences

Run-on sentences are independent clauses that have not been joined by a conjunction. When two or more independent clauses appear in one sentence, they must be joined in one of these ways:

1. Correction with a comma and a coordinating conjunction.

   Incorrect: I went on the trip and I had a good time.
   Correct: I went on the trip, and I had a good time.

2. Correction with a semicolon, a colon, or a dash. Used when independent clauses are closely related and their connection is clear without a coordinating conjunction.

   Incorrect: I went to the store and I bought some eggs.
   Correct: I went to the store; I bought some eggs.

3. Correction by separating sentences. This correction may be used when both independent clauses are long. Also, this can be used when one sentence is a question and one is not.

   Incorrect: The drive to New York takes ten hours it makes me very tired.
   Correct: The drive to New York takes ten hours. So, I become very tired.

4. Correction by changing parts of the sentence. One way is to turn one of the independent clauses into a phrase or subordinate clause.

   Incorrect: The drive to New York takes ten hours it makes me very tired.
   Correct: During the ten-hour drive to New York, I become very tired.

Note: Normally, one of these choices will be a clear correction to a run-on sentence. The fourth way can be the best correction but needs the most work.

Spelling

Rules of Spelling

Words Ending with a Consonant

Usually the final consonant is doubled on a word before adding a suffix. This is the rule for single syllable words, words ending with one consonant, and multi-syllable words with the last syllable accented. The following are examples:

- *beg* becomes *begging* (single syllable)
- *shop* becomes *shopped* (single syllable)
- *add* becomes *adding* (already ends in double consonant, do not add a third *d*)
- *deter* becomes *deterring* (multi-syllable, accent on last syllable)

- *regret* becomes *regrettable* (multi-syllable, accent on last syllable)
- *compost* becomes *composting* (do not add another *t* because the accent is on the first syllable)

Words Ending with Y or C

The general rule for words ending in *y* is to keep the *y* when adding a suffix if the *y* is preceded by a vowel. If the word ends in a consonant and *y* the *y* is changed to an *i* before the suffix is added (unless the suffix itself begins with *i*). The following are examples:

- *pay* becomes *paying* (keep the *y*)
- *bully* becomes *bullied* (change to *i*)
- *bully* becomes *bullying* (keep the *y* because the suffix is *–ing*)

If a word ends with *c* and the suffix begins with an *e, i,* or *y*, the letter *k* is usually added to the end of the word. The following are examples:

- panic becomes panicky
- mimic becomes mimicking

Words Containing IE or EI, and/or Ending with E

Most words are spelled with an *i* before *e*, except when they follow the letter *c*, **or** sound like *a*. For example, the following words are spelled correctly according to these rules:

- piece, friend, believe (*i* before *e*)
- receive, ceiling, conceited (except after *c*)
- weight, neighborhood, veil (sounds like *a*)

To add a suffix to words ending with the letter *e*, first determine if the *e* is silent. If it is, the *e* will be kept if the added suffix begins with a consonant. If the suffix begins with a vowel, the *e* is dropped. The following are examples:

- *age* becomes *ageless* (keep the *e*)
- *age* becomes *aging* (drop the *e*)

An exception to this rule occurs when the word ends in *ce* or *ge* and the suffix *able* or *ous* is added; these words will retain the letter *e*. The following are examples:

- courage becomes courageous
- notice becomes noticeable

Words Ending with ISE or IZE

A small number of words end with *ise*. Most of the words in the English language with the same sound end in *ize*. The following are examples:

- advertise, advise, arise, chastise, circumcise, and comprise
- compromise, demise, despise, devise, disguise, enterprise, excise, and exercise
- franchise, improvise, incise, merchandise, premise, reprise, and revise
- supervise, surmise, surprise, and televise

Words that end with *ize* include the following:

- accessorize, agonize, authorize, and brutalize
- capitalize, caramelize, categorize, civilize, and demonize
- downsize, empathize, euthanize, idolize, and immunize
- legalize, metabolize, mobilize, organize, and ostracize
- plagiarize, privatize, utilize, and visualize

(Note that some words may technically be spelled with *ise*, especially in British English, but it is more common to use *ize*. Examples include *symbolize/symbolise,* and *baptize/baptise.*)

Words Ending with CEED, SEDE, or CEDE

There are only three words that end with *ceed* in the English language: *exceed, proceed,* and *succeed.* There is only one word that ends with *sede,* and that word is *supersede.* Many other words that sound like *sede* actually end with *cede.* The following are examples:

- concede, recede, precede, and supercede

Words Ending in ABLE or IBLE

For words ending in *able* or *ible*, there are no hard and fast rules. The following are examples:

- adjustable, unbeatable, collectable, deliverable, and likeable
- edible, compatible, feasible, sensible, and credible

There are more words ending in *able* than *ible*; this is useful to know if guessing is necessary.

Words Ending in ANCE or ENCE

The suffixes *ence, ency,* and *ent* are used in the following cases:

- the suffix is preceded by the letter *c* but sounds like *s* – *innocence*
- the suffix is preceded by the letter *g* but sounds like *j* – *intelligence, negligence*

The suffixes *ance, ancy,* and *ant* are used in the following cases:

- the suffix is preceded by the letter *c* but sounds like *k* – *significant, vacant*
- the suffix is preceded by the letter *g* with a hard sound – *elegant, extravagance*

If the suffix is preceded by other letters, there are no steadfast rules. For example: *finance, elegance,* and *defendant* use the letter *a,* while *respondent, competence,* and *excellent* use the letter *e.*

Words Ending in TION, SION, or CIAN

Words ending in *tion, sion,* or *cian* all sound like *shun* or *zhun*. There are no rules for which ending is used for words. The following are examples:

- action, agitation, caution, fiction, nation, and motion
- admission, expression, mansion, permission, and television
- electrician, magician, musician, optician, and physician (note that these words tend to describe occupations)

Words with the AI or IA Combination

When deciding if *ai* or *ia* is correct, the combination of *ai* usually sounds like one vowel sound, as in *Britain*, while the vowels in *ia* are pronounced separately, as in *guardian*. The following are examples:

- captain, certain, faint, hair, malaise, and praise (*ai* makes one sound)
- bacteria, beneficiary, diamond, humiliation, and nuptial (ia makes two sounds)

Plural Forms of Nouns

Nouns Ending in CH, SH, S, X, or Z

When a noun ends in the letters *ch, sh, s, x,* or *z*, an *es* instead of a singular *s* is added to the end of the word to make it plural. The following are examples:

- church becomes churches
- bush becomes bushes
- bass becomes basses
- *mix* becomes *mixes*
- buzz becomes buzzes

This is the rule with proper names as well; the Ross family would become the Rosses.

Nouns Ending in Y or AY/EY/IY/OY/UY

If a noun ends with a consonant and y, the plural is formed by replacing the *y* with *ies*. For example, *fly* becomes *flies* and *puppy* becomes *puppies*. If a noun ends with a vowel and *y*, the plural is formed by adding an *s*. For example, *alley* becomes *alleys* and *boy* becomes *boys*.

Nouns Ending in F or FE

Most nouns ending in *f* or *fe* are pluralized by replacing the *f* with *v* and adding *es*. The following are examples:

- knife becomes knives; self becomes selves; wolf becomes wolves.

An exception to this rule is the word *roof; roof* becomes *roofs*.

Nouns Ending in O

Most nouns ending with a consonant and *o* are pluralized by adding *es*. The following are examples:

- hero becomes heroes; tornado becomes tornadoes; potato becomes potatoes

Most nouns ending with a vowel and *o* are pluralized by adding *s*. The following are examples:

- portfolio becomes portfolios; radio becomes radios; shoe becomes shoes.

An exception to these rules is seen with musical terms ending in *o*. These words are pluralized by adding *s* even if they end in a consonant and *o*. The following are examples: *soprano* becomes *sopranos; banjo* becomes *banjos; piano* becomes *pianos.*

Exceptions to the Rules of Plurals

Some words do not fall into any specific category for making the singular form plural. They are irregular. Certain words become plural by changing the vowels within the word. The following are examples:

- woman becomes women; goose becomes geese; foot becomes feet

Some words become completely different words in the plural form. The following are examples:

- mouse becomes mice; fungus becomes fungi; alumnus becomes alumni

Some words are the same in both the singular and plural forms. The following are examples:

- *Salmon, species,* and *deer* are all the same whether singular or plural.

Practice Questions

1. The police officer's manual can't cover every _______ situation; sometimes you'll just have to use your best judgment.

Which of these words would be the correct choice to fill in the blank?

a. conceivable
b. workable
c. dependable
d. reliable

2. Under no circumstances is it ever acceptible to wear a dirty or wrinkled uniform to work.

One word in the above sentence is misspelled. It is:

a. circumstances
b. acceptible
c. wrinkled
d. uniform

3. Officers must always be vigilant, as a tense situation can _______ suddenly.

Which of these words would be the correct choice to fill in the blank?

a. apprehend
b. escalate
c. insinuate
d. confabulate

4. The arguement between the two hostile inmates threatened to cause turmoil in the mess hall.

One word in the above sentence is misspelled. It is:

a. arguement
b. hostile
c. threatened
d. turmoil

5. If you always do the right thing, you never have to worry about a guilty _______.

Which of these words would be the correct choice to fill in the blank?

a. conscious
b. consciousness
c. concensus
d. conscience

Practice Answers

1. A: The word *conceivable* is the only choice for filling in the blank that makes any sense. Situations can't really be *workable, dependable,* or *reliable*. But they can be *conceivable*, which means something that can be thought of or imagined.

2. B: The word *acceptible* should be spelled *acceptable*. The other words are spelled correctly.

3. B: The word *escalate* is the only choice for filling in the blank that makes any sense. *Escalate* means to move fast, or quickly become worse. *Apprehend* means to catch. *Insinuate* means to hint at something bad without actually saying it. *Confabulate* means to make up stories that aren't true without being aware that you're doing so.

4. A: The word *arguement* should be spelled *argument*. The other words are spelled correctly.

5. D: The word *conscience* is the only choice for filling in the blank that makes any sense. *Conscience* refers to an inner sense of right and wrong; a person's views of the morality of his behavior. *Conscious* means aware of and responding to what's going on in the world, as opposed to unconscious (a person in a coma). *Consciousness* is simply the state of being conscious. *Consensus* means a kind of agreement between people.

Memorization

What Are These Questions Testing?

The questions in this section of the test measure your abilities at being able to note and recall specific information when necessary. In most cases, the information will be the sort of things you deal with every day—addresses, phone numbers, the make and model of a vehicle, names, faces, security codes, etc. Other information will be less common, but more important, such as a new assignment or a new shift.

What Is the Question Format?

On this section of the test, for each question, you will be shown a photo. You will be allowed to look at the picture for two minutes, in order to memorize as many details as you can about what's shown in the photo. After two minutes are up, you will no longer have access to the photo. Either it will disappear from your computer screen, or you will be required to turn the page in the test booklet. You will then have to answer some questions about the specific details in the photo, without being able to look at it.

What Strategies or Techniques Can I Use to Do Well on This Section?

The most important thing you can do to prepare for this section of the test is practice, practice, practice. Until they're tested on it, most people have no idea how difficult it is to recall facts and details from a picture they just looked at if it's taken away from them. As you will no doubt learn firsthand when you start working on the practice questions in this guide, it's not easy to look at a picture and memorize every single detail in two minutes.

However, the good news is that this is a skill that you can improve with practice. Not only can you improve it, you can see huge improvements in a short time span if you're diligent. To practice this skill effectively, you'll need another person. Find a friend, a loved one, or someone who is also prepping for the test and ask them to help you in this area.

You have plenty of material to work with—pick up any newspaper or magazine and you'll find lots of pictures you can use for this exercise. There are also tens of millions of photos of all kinds of things on the internet. Choose a picture, study it for two minutes, and then have your partner ask you some questions about the picture while you can't see it. Do this with several pictures each session. You'll be surprised at how much better you get, and how soon. But don't slack off, because this is an ability that you have to use regularly in order to maintain your skills. Practice on a regular basis right up until the day of your exam.

Practice Questions

Study the picture for two minutes. Then turn the page and answer some questions about the picture.

EXAMPLE PHOTO

1. How many people are shown in the photo?

a. 7
b. 6
c. 5
d. 4

2. How many of the men are NOT wearing a tie?

a. 1
b. 2
c. 3
d. 4

3. One of the men is wearing a flower in his lapel. It is the man who is:

a. First on the left
b. Second from the left
c. First on the right
d. Second from the right

4. How many of the men are wearing either a vest or a jacket in addition to a shirt?

a. 1
b. 2
c. 3
d. 4

5. Two of the men are holding something in their right hand. One man is holding something in his left hand. What is this man holding in his left hand?

a. A beverage in a bottle
b. A smartphone
c. A beverage in a glass
d. A small plate of dessert

Practice Answers

1. C: There are five people in the photo.

2. A: Four of the five men are wearing a tie; one is not.

3. D: The second man from the right is wearing a flower in his lapel.

4. B: The first man on the left is wearing a vest; the second man from the right is wearing a jacket.

5. C: The first man on the right is holding a beverage in a glass in his left hand.

Problem Sensitivity

What Are These Questions Testing?

Problem sensitivity is the ability to sense when there's a problem that isn't obvious, or when a seemingly calm situation is about to, or could very easily, turn into a serious problem. In these kinds of situations, you need the ability to recognize that "something's not right here" or "something's not adding up", even if you can't immediately identify what the problem is.

Everyone has some level of problem sensitivity, but people vary greatly in how much of this important skill they possess. This section of the test is designed to find out how much problem sensitivity you possess. It's important to note that these questions do not ask you to provide a solution to the problems you find, but only measure your abilities at noticing the problems.

What Is the Question Format?

There are several different kinds of Problem Sensitivity questions, and you may encounter some of each kind on your exam. For example, in one kind of question, you will be presented with a brief passage to read, which will describe a situation of the kind that is commonly encountered in law enforcement or corrections careers. You will be asked to select the answer which represents the main problem, or the most serious problem among several problems in the passage, or which one requires you to call for assistance to deal with it.

In another kind of question, you'll be given a rule or set of rules or procedures detailing how to handle certain situations, and then you'll be presented with a passage describing a situation and how it was handled. You'll be asked to decide what problem could arise from how the situation was handled. Or, you may be given a description of a situation and asked to choose the most appropriate action for an officer to take to deal with the situation.

Another common kind of question features statements from victims and or witnesses of a crime or an alleged crime. While none of the statements will match up exactly word for word with any of the others, one statement will be deliberately misleading, and you'll be asked to determine which statement is probably false.

What Strategies or Techniques Can I Use to Do Well on This Section?

As with the questions in the other sections, it's very important to take your time and read all of the information in each question thoroughly, without rushing through the passage. In many cases, selecting the correct answer will depend on noticing a fact or detail that could easily be overlooked by someone quickly skimming the passage.

Once you're sure you have thoroughly read the passage, think about the facts, details, and clues presented in the passage that can help you answer the question. Use your best judgment about how to deal with the situation and select your answer based on that.

Practice Questions

1. Parked beside a busy thoroughfare, you observe a blue sedan go by at very high speed. You turn on your lights and siren and pursue the car and it pulls over quickly. The driver is a young man of about 25 who apologizes and said he needs to get to the hospital right away as his wife has been in an accident. There is no odor of alcohol, his license is valid, and he has no warrants or prior arrests. The vehicle is registered to a woman with the same last name, which he says is his wife. What is the most likely explanation of his behavior?

a. His wife has been in an accident and he's rushing to the hospital
b. He was caught speeding and is lying in hopes of getting out of a ticket
c. He stole the car and got caught and is lying in hopes of getting out of being arrested
d. He is on drugs and is lying in hopes of getting out of being arrested

2. All of these calls came in around the same time on a Saturday afternoon. Which should receive the highest priority from police?

a. A caller says that his neighbor is blocking his driveway with his car
b. A caller reports that someone tried to break into his car earlier today
c. A convenience store owner reports that some inventory is missing from a storage room
d. A caller reports that two men are breaking into a junior high school

3. Which of these would normally be cause for further investigation?

a. A man in a parked car outside a bank at midnight
b. Two men walking down a neighborhood street at 9 PM
c. A man loading two cases of beer into his car trunk at a convenience store at 10 PM
d. Five teenagers hanging out at a park at 5 PM

4. At around 10 AM on a weekday morning, which is also the first day of school for the local district, you spot two boys who appear to be about 12 or 13 years old playing basketball in a public park. What is the most likely reason they're not in school?

a. They're homeschooled
b. They're skipping school
c. School was canceled
d. They're actually much older than they appear to be

5. A call comes in from a homeowner who is concerned about domestic violence at the house next door, 2215 Summerfield. He says it sounds like the man is beating his wife, but he doesn't want to get involved. You are dispatched to check it out. At the house at 2215 Summerfield, there are several cars in the driveway, and many more parked in the street. A man who identifies himself as the owner answers the door. You ask if you can speak to his wife. He calls her over, and she appears to be fine. You tell them you're there to check out a domestic dispute, and the man and the woman laugh. They tell you that they're getting ready for a football watching party and things got kind of loud, and they invite you in. In the living room, there are about a dozen adults snacking and watching TV. There doesn't appear to be anyone in danger. What's the best explanation for what happened?

a. The man was beating his wife, but they're both lying about it.
b. The neighbor has an axe to grind with these people and filed a false complaint as harassment
c. Another couple in the house was fighting and this is what the neighbor heard
d. The neighbor heard a loud party and misinterpreted things

Practice Answers

1. A: Going on the information you have available, the most likely scenario is that the driver's wife really has been in an accident and he's rushing to the hospital. There is nothing in this passage that suggests he appears to be under the influence of drugs or alcohol, so D is wrong. There's nothing to indicate the car has been reported stolen, so C should be discounted, even if it's theoretically possible. And while, B, that he is simply lying to get out of a speeding ticket is certainly possible, he has no warrants or prior arrests so it appears that he respects and obeys the law. Taking all these factors into consideration, it's most likely that he is telling the truth.

2. D: The call about two men breaking into a junior high school is the highest priority, as it's a crime in progress. All the other answer choices involve crimes that have already taken place. They certainly need investigating, but it's more important to attempt to stop a crime that's occurring at present.

3. A. While the other three answer choice scenarios depict people engaged in typical activities appropriate to the time and place, there are very few good reasons for a man to be sitting in a parked car outside a bank at midnight.

4. B: While the other three answers are theoretically possible, the most likely explanation is that the two boys are simply skipping school.

5. D: The most likely explanation is that the neighbor heard a loud party and misinterpreted things. While it's possible the man was beating his wife, or that another man was beating another woman, judging from the behavior and appearance of everyone in the house, neither one appears very probable. It's also possible that the neighbor filed a false report due to bad feelings between him and the homeowner, but without further evidence this theory should be discounted. Because parties do tend to get loud, and because there's no other evidence of anything being amiss, D is the most likely explanation.

Number Facility

The New York Civil Service exam measures the skills and aptitudes of job applicants in several different areas, and in the Number Facility section you'll be tested on your skills in math - addition, subtraction, division, multiplication, decimals, fractions, percents, etc. (The word *facility* usually refers to a room or a building, but it can also mean ability. That's how it's being used here.)

No matter what position you're applying for with the State of New York, you'll need math skills to carry out your job duties effectively and efficiently. You'll need to be able to add, subtract, multiply, and divide small numbers in your head without having to get out a pen and paper, or open your cell phone. You'll be using math every day you're on the job, and it's critical that you have these skills down pat before you get hired.

It's important to note that you won't be expected to have any advanced or college level math knowledge in order to do well on this part of the exam. You won't need to know calculus, geometry, trigonometry, statistics, etc. You'll only be required to demonstrate that you possess the knowledge and skills that everyone learns in junior high and high school.

In fact, according to the Department of Civil Service, you shouldn't even need to use a calculator to answer any of the questions. However, applicants who want to use a calculator during the Number Facility portion of the exam are allowed to bring one with them on test day, as long as they are small enough to fit in one's hand, quiet, and either solar-powered or battery-powered. It also can't have an alpha-numeric pad or keyboard. In other words, you can't have a cell phone, personal digital assistant, laptop, etc., in the testing room.

What Are These Questions Testing?

This section measures your ability to correctly perform mathematical operations involving integers, fractions, decimals, and percents. The mathematical operations used in these problems include addition, subtraction, multiplication, and division. As a result, you must be comfortable performing these four operations.

What Is the Question Format?

The questions will contain a simple arithmetic question and four answer options. Three of the answer choices will be incorrect, and one will be the correct answer. You must select the correct answer. It's important to take your time and double check your answers, if possible. It's likely that one or more of the wrong answer choices will be very similar to the correct answer, and you could easily choose the wrong one if you're in a rush.

Practice Questions

1. 4,307
+1,864

a. 5,161
b. 5,271
c. 6,171
d. 6,271

2. 707
x 17

a. 12,019
b. 12,049
c. 17,019
d. 17,049

3. $4\frac{1}{7} - 2\frac{1}{2} =$

a. $2\frac{5}{14}$
b. $1\frac{5}{14}$
c. $1\frac{9}{14}$
d. $2\frac{9}{14}$

4. Three eighths of forty equals:

a. 15
b. 20
c. 22
d. 24

5. 30% as a reduced common fraction

a. $\frac{30}{100}$
b. $\frac{1}{30}$
c. $\frac{23}{10}$
d. $\frac{3}{10}$

Practice Answers

1. C: This is a simple addition problem with carrying. Start with the ones column and add 7+4, write down the 1 and add the 1 to the digits in the tens column. Now add 0+6+1. Write down the 7. Now add 3+8 and write down the 1. Add the 1 to the thousands column. Add 4+1+1 and write the 6 to get the answer 6171.

2. A: This is a multiplication problem with 0. Start with the 7 in 17 and multiply it by each of the digits at the top 7×7. Write down the 9 and place the 4 in the ten's column. $7 \times 0 = 0$. Add the 4. $7 \times 7 = 49$. The top line will read 4949. Now multiply 1 by 7. Write down the 7. $1 \times 0 = 0$ and $1 \times 7 = 7$. The bottom line will read 707. Add these together with the 7 in the tens column and the answer will be 12,019.

$$\begin{array}{r} 707 \\ \times\ \ 17 \\ \hline \end{array} \qquad \begin{array}{r} {\scriptstyle +4} \\ 707 \\ \times\ \ 17 \\ \hline 4949 \end{array} \qquad \begin{array}{r} 707 \\ \times\ \ 17 \\ \hline 4949 \\ 707\ \end{array} \qquad \begin{array}{r} 707 \\ \times\ \ 17 \\ \hline 4949 \\ 707\ \\ \hline 12019 \end{array}$$

3. C: To subtract fractions, ensure that the denominator (the number on the bottom) is the same. Since it is not, change them both to 14ths. 17 equals 2/14. 1/2 equals 7/14. The equation now looks like this: $4\frac{3}{14} - 2\frac{7}{14}$. Change the 4 to 3 and add 14 to the numerator (the top number) so that the fractions can be subtracted. The equation now looks like this: $3\frac{16}{14} - 2\frac{97}{14}$. Subtract: $1\frac{9}{14}$

4. A: Divide 40 by 8 to get 5. Multiply 5 by 3 to get 15.

5. D: To solve, rewrite the percent as a fraction: $\frac{30}{100}$. Then reduce the fraction.

Mathematical Reasoning

It is vitally important that people hired for civil service jobs possess excellent basic math skills, which is why there are two separate sections covering these abilities on the New York Civil Service exam. Number Facility is one of the math portions of the exam, and Mathematical Reasoning is the other one.

Are These the Very Same Types of Questions as in the Number Facility Section?

No, although at first glance it may seem that way. Both sections contain questions involving basic math skills such as addition, subtraction, multiplication, and division. Questions involving percentages, decimals, and fractions are also featured in both sections. So, in that way, Number Facility and Mathematical Reasoning are very similar. However, the format of the questions in Mathematical Reasoning is very different than the question format in Number Facility.

In Number Facility, you will be presented with questions in pure math form. For example, you'll be asked what the product is when you multiply two numbers or what the sum of three numbers is. But in this section, the questions are in the form of word problems.

To solve word problems, you'll need problem interpretation skills alongside your pure math abilities.

The most important of these skills will be knowing which math function you'll need to use to solve the problem. Instead of being told to subtract one number from another, or divide one number by another, you'll have to be able to figure out what operations need to be performed and accurately perform the calculations to solve the problem.

What Are These Questions Testing?

Mathematical questions will generally take the form of a simple word problem. You will be posed an everyday situation that requires arithmetic to solve and asked to select the correct answer from the choices given. You may be asked to calculate rates, percentages, averages, or some other practical math quantity. You may also be asked to provide the expression needed to determine a solution. It is usually obvious what the question is asking for.

Practice Questions

1. One morning a total of 151 eggs are collected from a henhouse. The eggs are packed in cartons of 12 for shipment. How many eggs are remaining after as many cartons as possible are packed?

a. 3
b. 9
c. 7
d. 1

2. A rectangular plot in a garden is three times longer than it is wide. What is the perimeter of the garden if it has a width of 8 meters?

a. 32 meters
b. 192 meters
c. 24 meters
d. 64 meters

3. A bag full of C cookies is equally distributed among S students. Which expression correctly determines the number of cookies each student receives?

a. $C \div S$
b. $C \times S$
c. $C - S$
d. $S \div C$

4. Matthew wants to buy a video game that costs $25. He only has $18. How much additional money does Matthew need to save to purchase the game?

a. $7
b. $5
c. $8
d. $6

5. An electronics store sells *E* Evercell brand batteries in packages of 4 and *D* Durapower brand batteries in packages of 6. Which expression represents the total number of batteries in the store?

a. $(4 + E) \times (6 + D)$
b. $(4 \times E) + (6 \times D)$
c. $(4 + E) + (6 + D)$
d. $(4 \times E) \div (6 \times D)$

Practice Answers

1. C: The largest multiple of 12 less than 151 is 144. This means there are $151 - 144 = 7$ eggs left over.

2. D: A diagram of the plot would look like this:

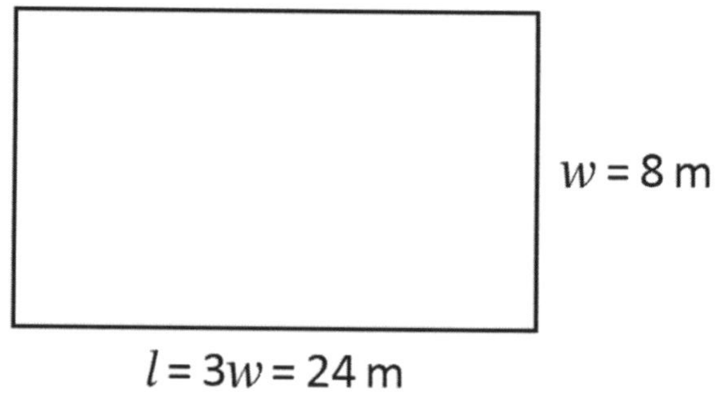

The perimeter of a rectangle is the formula $P = 2L + 2W$ which produces $2(24) + 2(8) = 48 + 16 = 64\,m$.

3. A: $C \div S$. Since the cookies are being divided up equally between the S students. Use some numbers to help see the correct answer. If $C = 40$ and $S = 10$.

$$C \div S = 40 \div 10 = 4$$

The incorrect choices produce the following with these values:

$$C \times S = 40 \times 10 = 400$$

$$C - S = 40 - 10 = 30$$

$$S \div C = 10 \div 40 = \frac{1}{4}$$

None of these seem reasonable.

4. A: This is a simple subtraction problem involving money. $25 -$18 = $7

5. B: The total number of Evercell batteries is $(4 \times E)$ and the total number of Durapower batteries is $(6 \times D)$. The sum of the two is the total number of batteries in the store.

Deductive Reasoning

What Are These Questions Testing?

There are several kinds of reasoning, but nearly all of them fall into one of the two big categories of reasoning—inductive and deductive. Inductive reasoning forms a generality from specifics. Deductive reasoning forms a specific from generalities. Deduction can be understood as applying a law, theory, or generality. This section of the test attempts to gauge your ability to apply a larger concept into a specific situation.

What Is the Question Format?

On this section of the test, you will be shown some written text, which will be some rules, laws, or regulations about a particular topic. Then you'll be presented with a situation, or scenario, and a question about how to apply the information you read to the scenario. Then you'll be shown several answer choices. Choosing the correct answer will require you to correctly interpret the information in the text and apply it to the scenario.

What Strategies or Techniques Can I Use to Do Well on This Section?

Once again, the most important strategy you can use in this section is to take the time to thoroughly read the information in the first part of the question that explains the rule, regulation, or law, and the scenario that calls for you to apply the information. You should have plenty of time to read the text and the scenario carefully, so try to avoid rushing. Many mistakes in this section can be avoided by simply reading carefully.

Once you've read the scenario, you'll want to look for clues in the text that can help you rule out obviously wrong answers. Words like *never, always, don't, must, should, shouldn't,* etc., can help you rule out some answer choices. Also, pay particular attention to words like *if, when, after, before,* etc., because these can provide strong clues to help you narrow down your answer if you still have two or three choices left after getting rid of answers that are obviously wrong.

Practice Questions

Here are some rules from the Police Officer Manual for a large city. Breaking any of these rules can result in receiving disciplinary action, up to and including being fired:

Rule 25: Failure to inventory and process recovered property in conformance with Department orders.

Rule 27: Disseminating, releasing, altering, defacing or removing any Department record or information concerning police matters except as provided by Department orders.

Rule 28: Participating in any partisan political campaign or activity.

Rule 29: Associating or fraternizing with any person known to have been convicted of any felony or misdemeanor, either State or Federal, excluding traffic and municipal ordinance violations.

Rule 30: Discussing bail with a person who is in custody except by those specifically authorized to let to bond.

Rule 32: Giving an opinion as to fine or penalty.

Rule 34: Recommending any professional or commercial service.

Rule 37: Advising any person engaged in a professional or commercial service that such professional or commercial services may be needed.

Rule 41: Soliciting or accepting any gratuity, or soliciting or accepting a gift, present, reward, or other thing of value for any service rendered as a Department member, or as a condition for the rendering of such service, or as a condition for not performing sworn duties.

1. You are a police officer who has sworn to follow the above rules. Your spouse is going to a fundraising event for a political campaign and is asking if you can come. You should:

a. Attend without offering money or services to the campaign
b. Request permission to attend from your superior officer
c. Explain that you cannot attend the event
d. Attend, because you will not be on duty

2. You are a police officer who has sworn to follow the above rules. You answer a call about a break-in at a jewelry shop. You arrive to find that the owner of the shop has pepper-sprayed the burglar. As you apprehend the suspect, the owner hands you a watch in thanks for your help. You return the watch with an explanation that you are not allowed to receive gifts. Have you broken rule 41 from the manual?

a. Yes, the offer of the watch has invalidated your judgement
b. No, because you have not accepted the gift, you have not broken the rule
c. It depends on whether you feel the offer affected your decision to arrest the suspect
d. Only if you must take the owner's word on the burglary

3. Which of the following would be cause for disciplinary action?

a. Donating money to a political party
b. Writing an anonymous letter to the press with details on a confidential case
c. Joining a poker group with someone previously convicted for operating an unlicensed vehicle
d. Receiving a housewarming gift when moving into a new neighborhood

Money Laundering:

(a) A person commits an offense if the person knowingly:

(1) acquires or maintains an interest in, conceals, possesses, transfers, or transports the proceeds of criminal activity;

(2) conducts, supervises, or facilitates a transaction involving the proceeds of criminal activity;

(3) invests, expends, or receives, or offers to invest, expend, or receive, the proceeds of criminal activity or funds that the person believes are the proceeds of criminal activity; or

(4) finances or invests or intends to finance or invest funds that the person believes are intended to further the commission of criminal activity.

(a-1) Knowledge of the specific nature of the criminal activity giving rise to the proceeds is not required to establish a culpable mental state under this section.

(b) It is a defense to prosecution under this section that the person acted with intent to facilitate the lawful seizure, forfeiture, or disposition of funds or other legitimate law enforcement purpose pursuant to the laws of this state or the US

(c) It is a defense to prosecution under this section that the transaction was necessary to preserve a person's right to representation as guaranteed by the Sixth Amendment of the United States Constitution and by Article 1, Section 10, of the Texas Constitution or that the funds were received as bona fide legal fees by a licensed attorney and at the time of their receipt, the attorney did not have actual knowledge that the funds were derived from criminal activity.

(d) An offense under this section is:

(1) a state jail felony if the value of the funds is $2,500 or more but less than $30,000;

(2) a felony of the third degree if the value of the funds is $30,000 or more but less than $150,000;

(3) a felony of the second degree if the value of the funds is $150,000 or more but less than $300,000; or

(4) a felony of the first degree if the value of the funds is $300,000 or more.

4. A jeweler is negotiating a deal for the sale of over $45,000 in precious stones and jewels. During the trade, the customer mentions in confidence that the money offered in payment has come from an unspecified illegal activity. The jeweler doesn't notify anyone of the fact and finishes the deal. Which of the following describes the jeweler's situation?

a. Because the jeweler knowingly aided in a transaction with the proceeds of criminal activity, he has committed an offense.
b. Because the jeweler has only performed his job in a normal fashion, he has not committed an offense.
c. Because the jeweler has not received any abnormal benefit from the exchange, the jeweler has not committed an offense.
d. Because the jeweler does not know what crime the customer has committed, the jeweler has not committed an offense.

5. Which of the following would be a second degree felony?

a. Investing $180,000 in stocks and bonds for a non-profit organization
b. Selling a gold watch found on the street for $2,000
c. Working with an offshore bank to move $350,000 into a more reputable and lawful bank account for an identity theft group
d. Selling a house to a drug dealer for $200,000 in dirty money

Practice Answers

1. C: You should explain that you cannot attend the event. Rule 28 prohibits participating in a political fundraiser.

2. B: Because you have not accepted or solicited the gift, you have not broken rule 41.

3. B: Releasing information concerning police matters on confidential cases is prohibited by rule 27. Rule 28 does not prohibit donation of money to political parties. Rule 29 does not prohibit associating or fraternizing with a person known to be convicted of traffic and municipal ordinance violations. Rule 41 does not prohibit accepting gifts not associated with the performing of duties as a police officer.

4. A: The person has facilitated a transaction involving the proceeds of criminal activity which is prohibited under rule (2)(a). Guilt of money laundering does not depend on whether the suspect performs his job as normal, receives abnormal benefits, or knows the specific nature of the criminal activity giving rise to the proceeds.

5. D: Selling a house for $200,000 of dirty money is a felony of the second degree. Option C is also illegal, but would be a felony of the first degree. Options A and B are not felonies.

Inductive Reasoning

What Are These Questions Testing?

There are two mains kinds of reasoning –deductive, and inductive. Inductive reasoning forms a generality from specifics. Deductive reasoning forms a specific from generalities. Much of the reasoning we use throughout the day is inductive. You can compare inductive reasoning to putting together a puzzle—you use little bits of pieces here and there, you notice patterns, you match up a piece with a slot, and you build the whole from individual pieces. That's inductive reasoning—working from individual, specific pieces of information to form a larger conclusion.

What Is the Question Format?

On this section of the test, you will be shown a set of data that is displayed in a visual format, usually a table, pie graph, or bar graph. Then you'll answer a question which will require you to interpret the visual data and draw a conclusion based on it.

What Strategies or Techniques Can I Use to Do Well on This Section?

As is the case with every section of the test, one of the most important strategies is reading carefully. Even though the information will be presented in visual form, there will be written text explaining what each element of the table, chart, or graph represents. It's very important that you take enough time to make sure you understand every element of the data you're looking at.

Practice Questions

1. Here are two pie charts about the most recent class to graduate from a city police academy, breaking them down by sex and educational level.

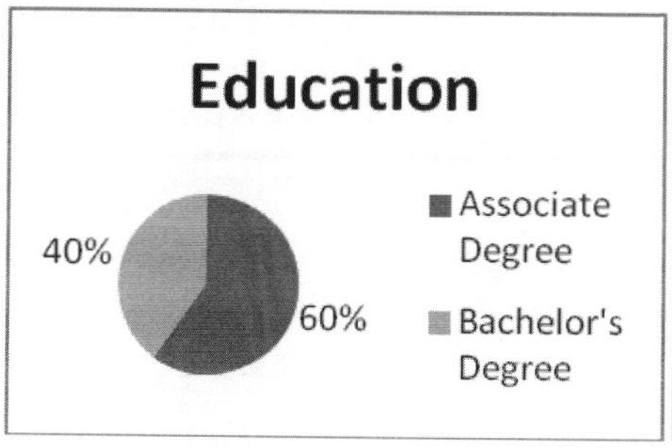

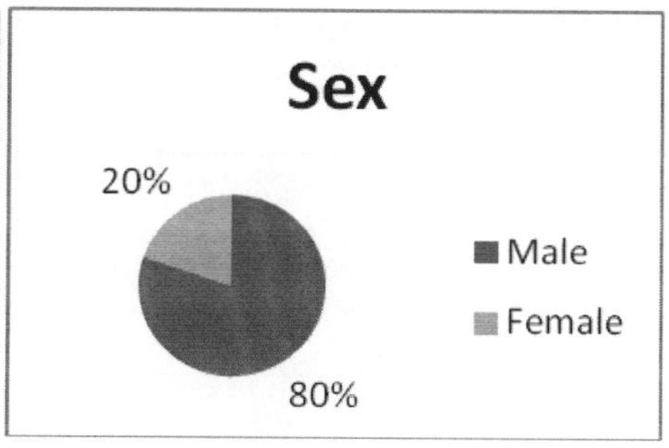

There were one hundred graduates. Half of the female graduates possess a bachelor's degree. How many of the male graduates have a bachelor's degree?

a. 20
b. 25
c. 30
d. 35

2. This table shows the number of times corrections officers called off sick for a shift at four different facilities. The middle column is the number of call-offs in September. The right column represents the number of call-offs in October, when the flu was going around. Assuming that the number of call-offs in September is fairly typical for a normal month, which facility's corrections staff appears to have been least affected by the flu virus?

Facility	September call-offs	October call-offs
Milton	9	12
Ferguson	12	18
Dalton	17	15
Howard	2	6

a. Milton
b. Ferguson
c. Dalton
d. Howard

3. An increasing number of cities are drafting new regulations concerning tattoos on police officers. Up until a couple of decades ago, very few people had tattoos. Among people that were tattooed, most only had one and it was small and covered by clothing. On top of that, the vast majority of people who had a tattoo weren't interested in becoming police officers. Until recently, therefore, many cities had no official policy concerning tattoos on police officers because it was a situation that rarely came up. These days, however, tattoos are much more common, and many people have several, and it's not unusual for these tattoos to be visible even when the person is fully clothed. Here is a table with the number of officers in one county sheriff's department who have 1, 2, 3, or 4+ tattoos, by age range:

Age	1 Tattoo	2 Tattoos	3 Tattoos	4+ Tattoos
22 to 30	15	10	5	1
31 to 45	10	7	5	3
46 to 54	5	5	2	0
55+	3	1	0	0

How many people in the department have at least two tattoos?

a. 33
b. 35
c. 37
d. 39

4. Some small towns and villages located near interstate freeways take advantage of that fact by creating speed traps. That is, they set a lower speed limit on the part of the freeway that falls in their jurisdiction. The speed limit changes without warning and for no apparent reason. Many unsuspecting motorists never see the sign about the lower speed limit, or they see it too late, and are essentially tricked into exceeding the artificially low speed limit. The motorists are then pulled over and issued a speeding ticket. For some of these towns, speeding tickets bring in the majority of the local government's revenue. Some state governments are cracking down on this practice, by limiting the percentage of a town's budget that can come from speeding tickets to no more than 30%, and requiring the towns to turn over any amount exceeding that to the state. Here is a chart showing the percentage of municipal revenue brought in by speeding tickets in one state's worst speed traps, before and after the state passed the law capping speeding ticket revenues.

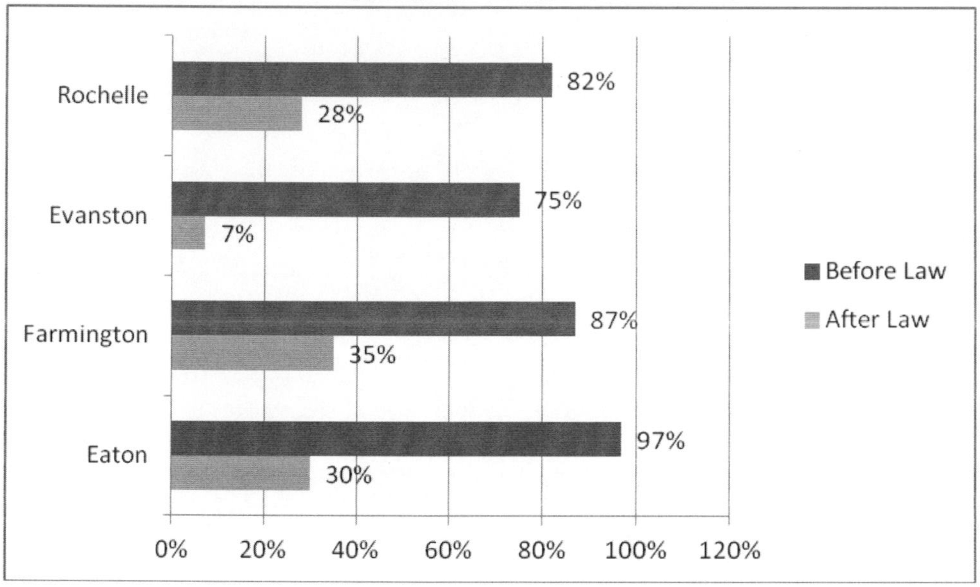

As a percentage, which town had the biggest drop in their revenue from speeding tickets?

a. Rochelle
b. Evanston
c. Farmington
d. Eaton

5. Here is a table showing the number and kinds of contraband items confiscated last week at four facilities.

Facility	Drugs	Phone	Weapon	Tobacco
Lancaster	3	8	7	12
Charleston	9	1	0	9
Hartwig	12	6	9	2
Wharton	7	9	8	7

Which facility had the most contraband items confiscated last week?

a. Lancaster
b. Charleston
c. Hartwig
d. Wharton

Practice Answers

1. C: 40% of 100 is 40, so a total of 40 graduates hold a bachelor's degree. 20% of the graduates are women, and half of them have a bachelor's. Half of 20 is 10. If 40 of the graduates have a bachelor's degree, and women have 10, then 30 men have a bachelor's degree.

2. C: Of the four facilities, three had more call-offs in October than in September, but Dalton had fewer. It stands to reason that they weren't as affected by the flu virus.

3. D: To find the correct answer, simply add up all the numbers in the 2, 3, and 4 Tattoo columns, and the total is the correct answer, 39.

4. B: You can do the math using the same formula used in Questions 9 and 13, but that shouldn't be necessary. It should be pretty clear with just a glance that the city of Evanston experienced a far bigger percentage drop in revenue than the other three towns.

5. D: To answer this question, simply add up the number of items in all four categories, for each city, and that's the total number of contraband items confiscated last week. Lancaster had 30, Charleston had 19, Hartwig had 29, and Wharton had 31.

Information Ordering

What Are These Questions Testing?

The Information Ordering section of the test tests your abilities to think quickly and logically about ordering and progression.

What Is the Question Format?

You will be shown several pieces of related information (usually 5-6 numbered items). Often they will be rules to follow in certain situations, description of a series of actions or events, or instructions for accomplishing a certain task. In most questions, the different pieces of information will be out of logical or chronological order. In that case, you will be shown answer choices with the numbered items in various orders, and you'll be required to select the answer that has the items in the correct logical or chronological order. Other questions may feature items that are already in order, and require you to answer a question that demonstrates that you have correctly grasped the order the items are in by requiring you to decide in which step something happened, or should take place.

What Strategies or Techniques Can I Use to Do Well on This Section?

A critical factor in doing well on Information Ordering questions is reading carefully. Don't rush through and merely skim the list of items; slow down and read thoroughly so you understand what's going on in each step. It's also important to read all of the items before looking at the answer choices and note which item should be first on the list. That will help you eliminate wrong answers quickly. Once you know which numbered item should be at the beginning, any answer choice that doesn't have the correct item in the first position can be eliminated.

Reading the items first becomes even more effective if you can remember not only which item should be first on the list, but also which one should be last, as this will also allow you to eliminate any questions which have the wrong item in the last position.

If you're having any trouble putting the items in order, use context clues to help you. Sometimes items will include words such as *next, then, or after*. If an item contains a word or phrase like these, then it cannot be first. By the same logic, if an item contains a word or phrase such as *start* or *begin by* ____, it almost certainly should be the first item on the list.

Also, if you're having trouble putting the items in the proper order, you can try starting backward—decide which item should be last and work in reverse from there. Sometimes this different perspective will make things clearer.

Practice Questions

1. If officers arrive at the scene of a crime and have reason to believe it was motivated by bias, they should notify the Hate Crimes Unit (HCU) at once. The HCU supervisor is to follow these procedures. Put them in the correct order:

1. After victim and witness interviews, determine the seriousness of the incident and make appropriate notifications.
2. Report to the scene immediately.
3. Arrange for an increase of patrols throughout the affected area for the foreseeable future.
4. Complete an After Action Report detailing events and actions taken by HCU and PD.
5. Interview the victim(s) as soon as possible, at the scene or at the hospital, and assure them that the investigation will be actively pursued.

a. 1,2,5,3,4
b. 2,5,1,3,4
c. 2,1,5,3,4
d. 3,1,2,5,4

2. Rules for conducting strip searches:

1. Station another officer just outside the location of the search to be on standby in case of trouble.
2. The officer administering the search should never put their finger or any other object into an inmate's orifice while conducting a strip search.
3. If the officer sees what appears to be contraband in the inmate's orifice (vaginal or anal cavity), the officer should ask the inmate to remove the object.
4. If the inmate refuses to remove the object, the officer shouldn't attempt to remove it. A body cavity search warrant will have to be approved in order to remove the item.
5. Once an inmate refuses to remove the item, the officer should end the strip search immediately and follow the procedures for requesting the approval of a body cavity search warrant.

If the officer who observes contraband in an inmate's orifice attempts to remove it himself after the inmate refuses to remove it, he has violated which of the above procedures?

a. 2,4,5
b. 1,2,3
c. 2,3,4
d. 3,4,5

3. Your department encourages citizens to take part in the Neighborhood Block Watch program. You are the community liaison officer in charge of coordinating the Neighborhood Watch and having signs put up announcing that an area participates in the program. Put these steps of the process in order.

1. Determine the best location for the sign.
2. Verify that at least 50% of community members have agreed to be active members of the Block Watch.
3. Send a job request to Traffic and Road Operations to install the sign.
4. Accept the application from a representative of the neighborhood.
5. If 50% of community members have agreed to take part, approve the application.

a. 1,2,4,5,3
b. 4,2,5,1,3
c. 4,1,2,5,3
d. 3,4,1,5,2

4. Law enforcement agencies, like other government agencies, are often required by law to release certain records or other public information. Units and sections do not make the decisions about releasing records; all decisions are made by the Records Unit. If the Records Unit contacts your unit or section and requests copies of certain records, these are the steps to follow.

1. Send the copy to the Records Unit.
2. Determine if the record is available. If so, proceed with the next step. If not, fill out Form 204-B and send to the Records Unit.
3. Place a memo documenting your compliance with the request in the Records Request file.
4. On the copy you've made, black out any information as needed to comply with privacy laws (see sections 3.21 and 3.22).
5. Make a copy of the record.

Place the steps in order.

a. 2,5,4,1,3
b. 2,5,1,4,3
c. 5,2,1,3,4
d. 3,2,5,1,4

5. Here are some of the rules governing the use of Marine Patrols outside of city limits.

1. Approval can only be given by a captain or higher, if available.
2. If a captain or higher is not available, the Marine Patrol Unit Officer-in-Charge may give approval.
3. If the Marine Patrol Unit Officer-in-Charge is not available, a Marine Patrol supervisor may give approval.
4. During any such use, an officer for the agency who requested the Marine Patrol must be onboard at all times to carry out enforcement actions.
5. Only certified Marine Patrol operators are allowed to navigate the vessel.

An officer of the requesting agency:

a. Can give approval if a captain or higher isn't available.
b. Must navigate the vessel if a certified Marine Patrol operator isn't available.
c. Must be on board at all times.
d. Can override the decision of a Marine Patrol Unit Officer-in-Charge who refuses to give approval.

Practice Answers

1. B: The correct order is 2,5,1,3,4. 2) Report to the scene immediately. 5) Interview the victim(s) as soon as possible, at the scene or at the hospital, and assure them that the investigation will be actively pursued. 1) After victim and witness interviews, determine the seriousness of the incident and make appropriate notifications. 3) Arrange for an increase of patrols throughout the affected area for the foreseeable future. 4) Complete an After Action Report detailing events and actions taken by HCU and PD.

2. A: The officer has violated rules 2, 4, and 5. Rule 2 states that an officer should never insert a finger or other object into an inmate's orifice. Rule 4 says that even if the inmate refuses to remove the object, the officer is not to attempt to remove it. Rule 5 states that the next step after an inmate refuses to remove an object is for the officer to request the approval of a body search. Rule 1 doesn't have any bearing on this question. Rule 3 says that an officer should ask the inmate to remove an item discovered in a cavity search, which the officer in this hypothetical situation did, so it was not violated.

3. B: The correct order is 4,2,5,1,3. 4) Accept the application from a representative of the neighborhood. 2) Verify that at least 50% of community members have agreed to be active members of the Block Watch. 5) If 50% of community members have agreed to take part, approve the application. 1) Determine the best location for the sign. 3) Send a job request to Traffic and Road Operations to install the sign.

4. A: The correct order is 2,5,4,1,3. 2) Determine if the record is available. If so, proceed with the next step. If not, fill out Form 204-B and send to the Records Unit. 5) Make a copy of the record. 4) On the copy you've made, black out any information as needed to comply with privacy laws (see sections 3.21 and 3.22). 1) Send the copy to the Records Unit. 3) Place a memo documenting your compliance with the request in the Records Request file.

5. C: Rule 4 states that an officer for the agency who requested the Marine Patrol must be onboard at all times. However, none of the rules state that an officer for the agency who requested can give approval, navigate the vessel, or override the decision of a Marine Patrol Unit Officer-in-Charge who refuses to give approval.

Spatial Orientation

What is the Question Format?

For the questions in this section, you will be shown a map, along with a compass or an indicator of which direction is north. You will then be given a scenario below the map. The scenario will state the location of an officer (or officers) and describe a situation that has come up requiring the officer(s) to proceed to a different location, which will also be stated. While both locations are stated in the scenario, neither location is pinpointed on the map. You will be required to choose the answer selection that describes the shortest route between the two locations.

What Strategies or Techniques Can I Use to Do Well on This Section?

As with the questions in all the sections, it's very important that you take the time to read the question carefully. Pay very close attention to the current location of the officer(s), and also to the second location. Find each one on the map before looking at the answer choices.

Once you've pinpointed both locations, start considering each answer choice. Unlike with many multiple-choice questions, where you can often see that one answer is obviously correct, and ignore the other answer choices, on these questions, you won't be able to do that. Because you're looking for the shortest route, you will need to read, consider, and compare each answer choice. As you read the route in each answer choice, look at the map to visually follow the route. Then select the one that involves the least distance between the two points.

If you think you need practice before the day of your test, you can stop using your GPS or computer for directions, and rely on an old-fashioned map to find the way to some areas you're unfamiliar with. This will help you become more comfortable with map-reading.

Practice Questions

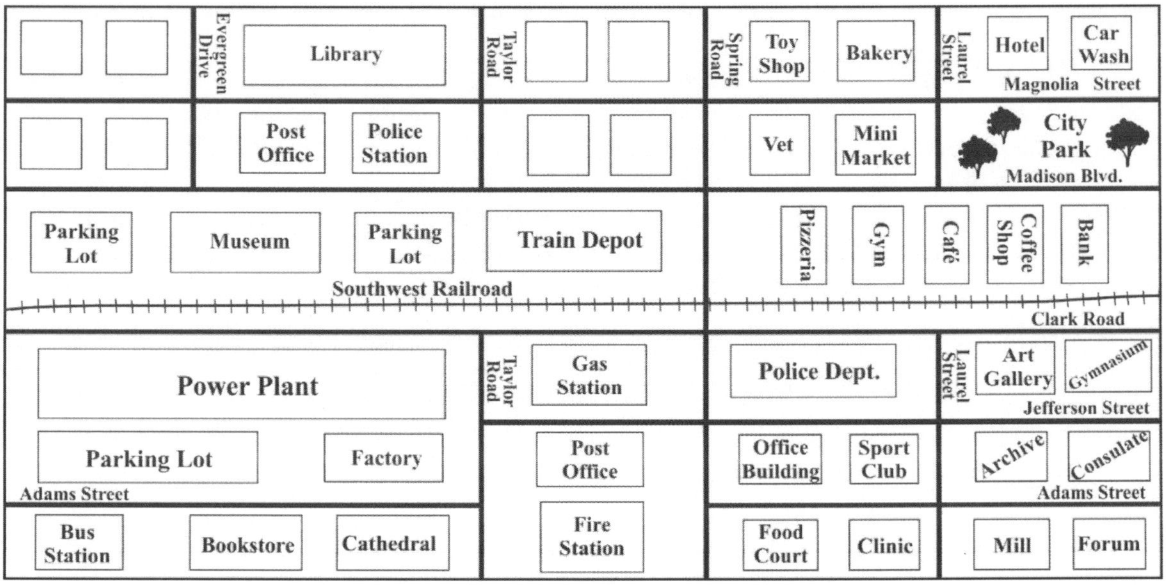

1. An officer is parked between the factory and the post office, and needs to get to the bakery to take a report of a person who stole some merchandise. Which of these would be the shortest route between her current location and the bakery?

a. Drive south on Taylor Road, and west on Adams Street.
b. Drive south on Taylor Road, north on Spring Road, and east on Magnolia Street.
c. Drive north on Taylor Road, east on Jefferson Street, and North on Laurel Street.
d. Drive north on Taylor Road, east on Jefferson Street, north on Spring Road, and east on Magnolia Street.

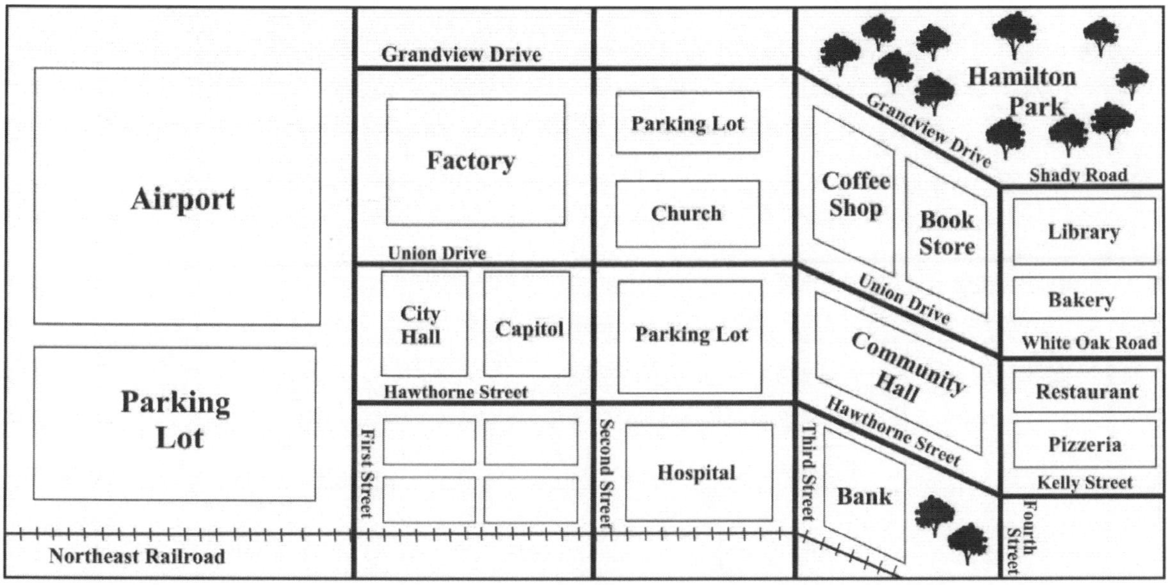

2. If an officer is patrolling Grandview Drive in front of the factory, which of these is his fastest route to the intersection of Kelly Street and Fourth Street?

a. Drive west on Grandview Drive and south on Fourth Street.
b. Drive east on Grandview Drive and south on Fourth Street.
c. Drive east on Grandview Drive and south on Kelly Street.
d. Drive west on Grandview drive and south on First Street.

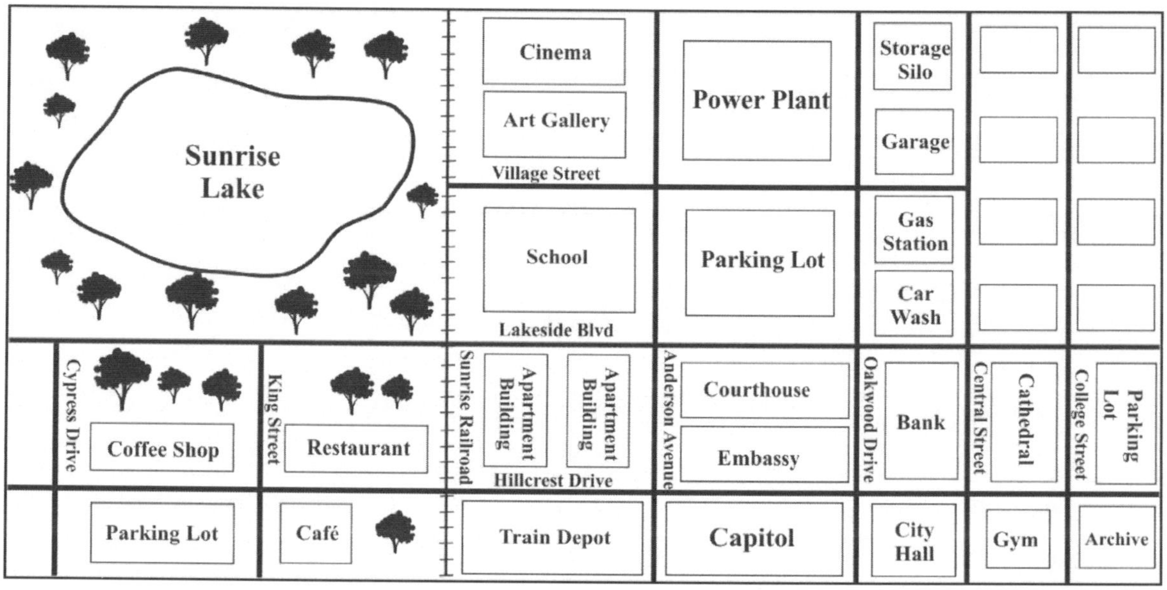

3. Officer Robinson is in the parking lot across from the coffee shop when he is dispatched to the gas station to investigate a fight at the gas station. However, Hillcrest Drive is blocked off in front of the embassy. What is the shortest alternative route for him to take to the gas station?

a. Drive east on Hillcrest Drive, north on Anderson Avenue, and east on Village Street.
b. Drive west on Hillcrest Drive, north on Cypress Drive, and east on Lakeside Boulevard.
c. Drive east on Hillcrest Drive, north on King Street, east on Lakeside Boulevard, and north on College Street.
d. Drive east on Hillcrest Drive, and north on Central Street.

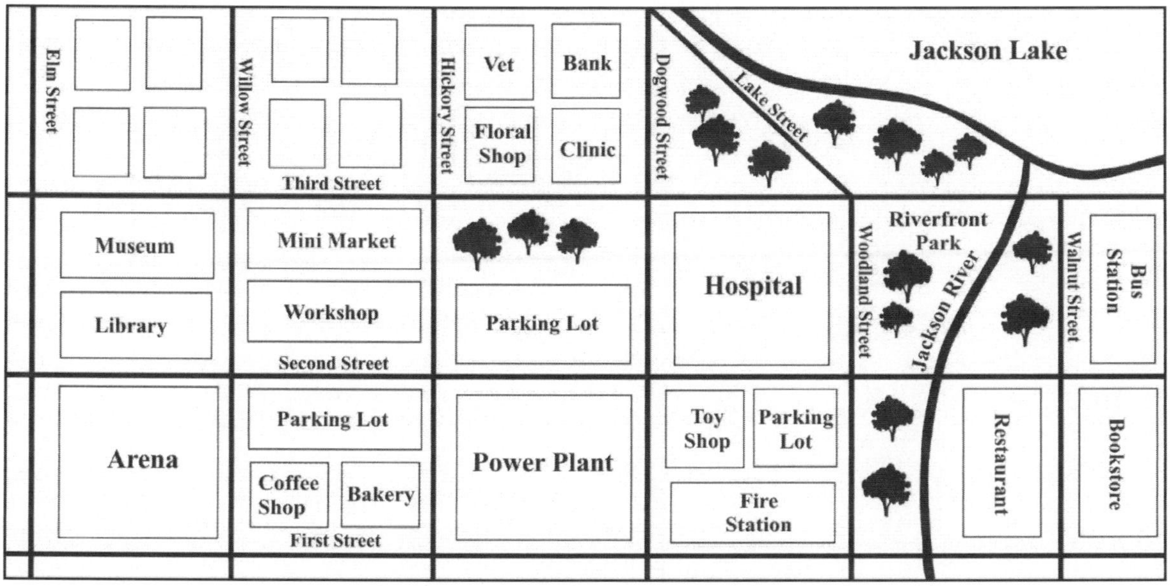

4. Two officers are on late night patrol between the bus station and Jackson River, when they are dispatched to investigate a suspicious person seen loitering near the bank. Which of these routes will involve traveling the shortest distance to get to the bank?

a. Drive north on Walnut Street, west on Third Street, and north on Hickory Street.
b. Drive north on Walnut Street, west on Third Street, and north on Dogwood Street.
c. Drive south on Walnut Street, west on Second Street, and north on Hickory Street.
d. Drive south on Walnut Street, west on Second Street, and north on Dogwood Street.

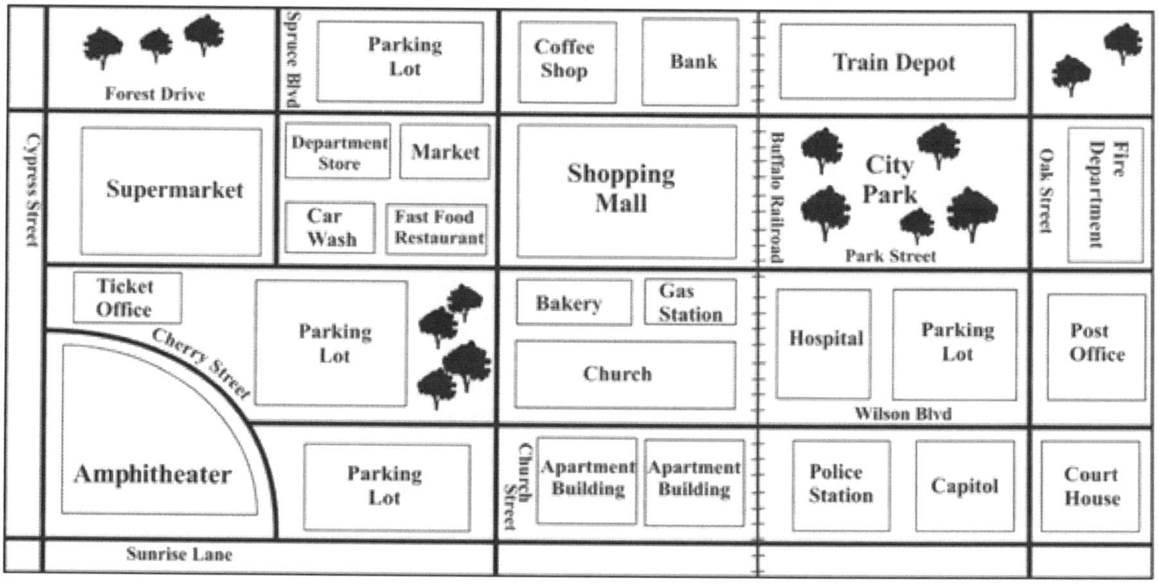

5. An officer is in his patrol car, between the church and the apartment buildings. He needs to respond to a call at the department store. Which of these is the shortest route between his current location and the department store?

a. Drive west on Wilson Boulevard, north on Church Street, and west on Forest Drive.
b. Drive west on Wilson Boulevard, north on Church Street, west on Park Street, north on Cypress Street, and east on Forest Drive.
c. Drive west on Sunrise Lane, north on Church Street, and west on Forest Drive.
d. Drive north on Church Street and west on Forest Drive.

Practice Answers

1. D: Drive north on Taylor Road, east on Clark Road, north on Spring Road, and east on Magnolia Street. *A* and *B* are both wrong right off the bat, because heading south on Taylor Road would be going in the wrong direction. C is wrong because going north on Taylor Road won't take the officer to Jefferson Street, which is south of Taylor Road. Also, taking Jefferson Street to Laurel Street is impossible, as the two streets don't connect.

2. B: Drive east on Grandview Drive and south on Fourth Street. *A* is wrong because going west on Grandview Drive would be going in the wrong direction. *D* is wrong for the same reason, and because going south on First would take the officer nowhere near the desired destination. *C* is incorrect, because going south on Kelly Street is impossible, as it runs east to west, and Grandview Drive doesn't connect to Kelly Street, either.

3. A: Drive east on Hillcrest Drive, north on Anderson Avenue, and east on Village Street. *B* is incorrect because west on Hillcrest Drive would be the opposite direction the officer needs to be going. *C* is incorrect because it goes past the destination—if the officer went east all the way to College Street, he would have gone too far, and would have to turn around and backtrack a few blocks. *D* is wrong because the officer can't reach Central Street by going east on Hillcrest Drive, because the question says that Hillcrest is blocked off in front of the embassy. (If traffic weren't blocked in front of the embassy, *D* would be the shortest route.)

4. B: Drive north on Walnut Street, west on Third Street, and north on Dogwood Street. *A* is wrong because driving to Hickory Street before turning north would be going past the bank, and the officers would have to turn around and backtrack. *C* is wrong because the officers need to go north on Walnut Street, not south, and Hickory Street is not the street the bank is located on. *D* is wrong because the officers need to go north on Walnut Street, not south.

5. A: Drive west on Wilson Boulevard, north on Church Street, and west on Forest Drive. *B* is incorrect as turning west on Park Street will take the office far out of the way he should be going, requiring him to do a lot of unnecessary driving to reach the store. *C* is wrong because it has the officer beginning on Sunrise Lane, when he is actually on Wilson Boulevard. *D* is incorrect because the officer is on Wilson Boulevard, so his first action can't be driving north on Church Street.

Visualization

The ability to visualize things, that is, the ability to create an accurate mental picture of a physical object without actually being able to see the object, is a skill that will prove useful in many different occupations.

It's possible that you have never encountered visualization questions before. If that's the case, you will find that these questions don't look anything like most questions you'll find in a standardized test. To do well on these questions, you'll want to take your time and study the original illustration before trying to decide which of the other illustrations shows it from a different angle.

Visualization is more of an aptitude than a learned skill – some people are naturally better at it than other people are. However, no matter how good you are at visualization right now, you'll almost certainly get better with practice. Take advantage of the practice questions in this guide, and you can improve your chances of making a great score in this section.

What Are These Questions Testing?

These questions are designed to test your spatial and geometric ability. In particular, they test your ability to recognize objects when they are shown from a different orientation or after unfolding.

What Is the Question Format?

Because visualization is varied in theory and application, it can be tested in different ways. However, all problems will use the same two concepts: rotation and folding.

Rotation

The test will show a picture of a three-dimensional block, and several possible answer choices. One of the answer choices shows the same block as the original, but rotated. You will have to identify which of the answer choices is the same.

Unfolding

A flat square of paper is folded one or more times. The broken lines indicate the original position of the paper. The solid lines indicate the position of the folded paper. The paper is never turned or twisted. The folded paper always remains within the edges of the original square. There are multiple folds in each item. After the last fold, a hole is punched in the paper. Your task is to mentally unfold the paper and determine the position of the holes on the original square. Choose the pattern of black circles that indicates the position of the holes on the original square. There is only one correct pattern for each item.

You are always provided with multiple drawings: the first fold, then the second fold, then the third if necessary. After looking at where the hole punch is, mentally draw on top of the drawing of the second fold what the hole punches would look like at that stage. This makes it easier to determine what they would look like once the paper is completely unfolded.

Practice Questions

In the pictures below, which of the answer choices shows the same block as the original?

1.

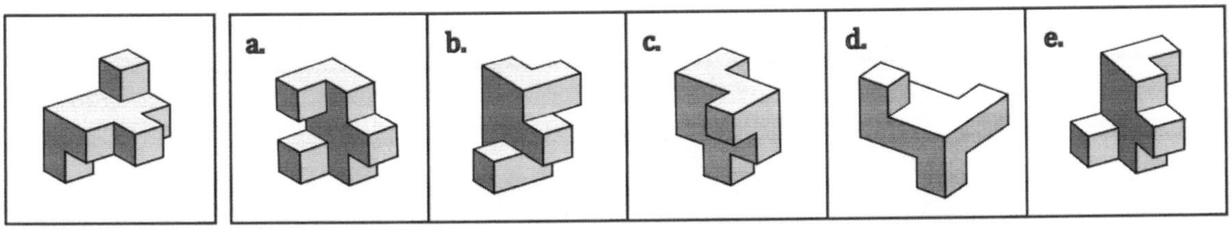

2.

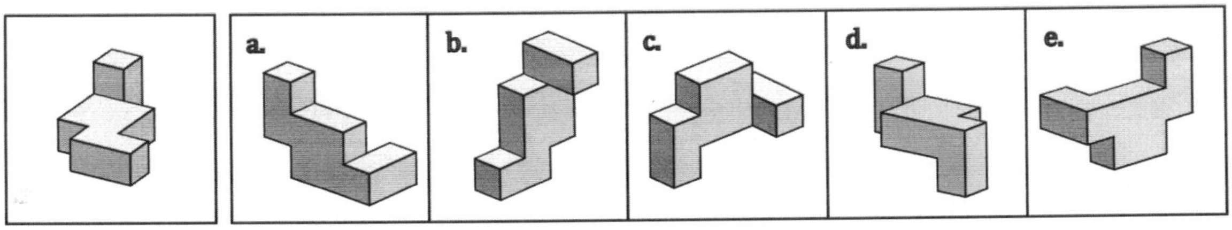

3.

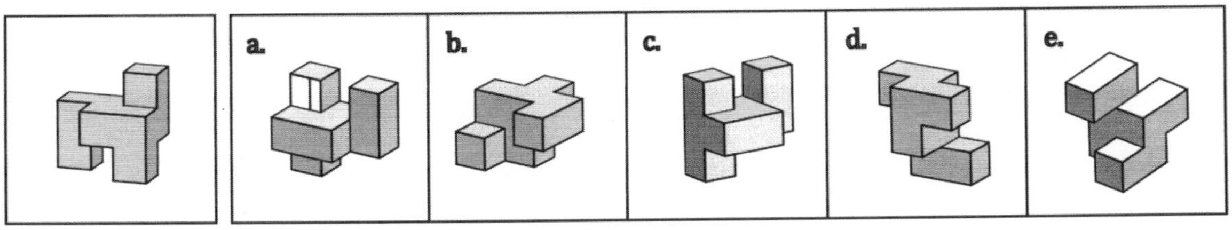

A flat square of paper is folded one or more times. The broken lines indicate the original position of the paper. The solid lines indicate the position of the folded paper. The paper is never turned or twisted. The folded paper always remains within the edges of the original square. There are multiple folds in each item. After the last fold, a hole is punched in the paper. Your task is to mentally unfold the paper and determine the position of the holes on the original square. Choose the pattern of black circles that indicates the position of the holes on the original square. There is only one correct pattern for each item.

4.

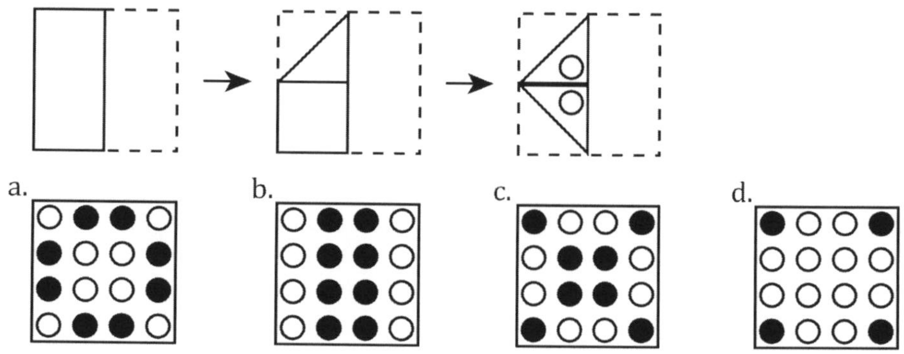

5.

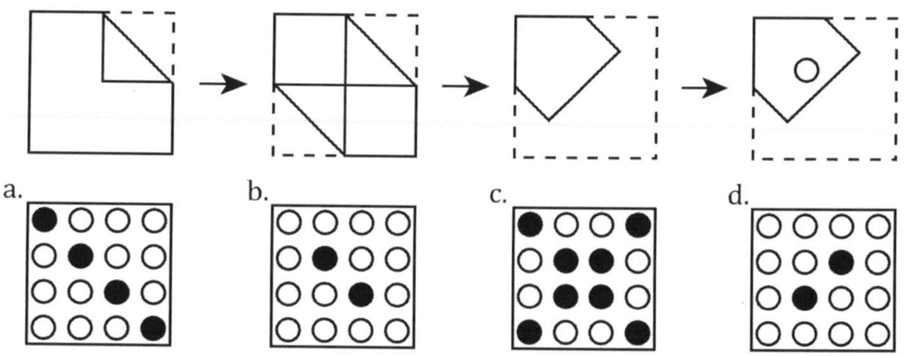

Practice Answers

1. C: Option A is wrong because there are two protrusions on one side of the block, instead of one protrusion on each side like in the example block. Options B, D and E are also wrong because the protrusions are on the wrong part of the block.

2. A:

3. D:

4. C:

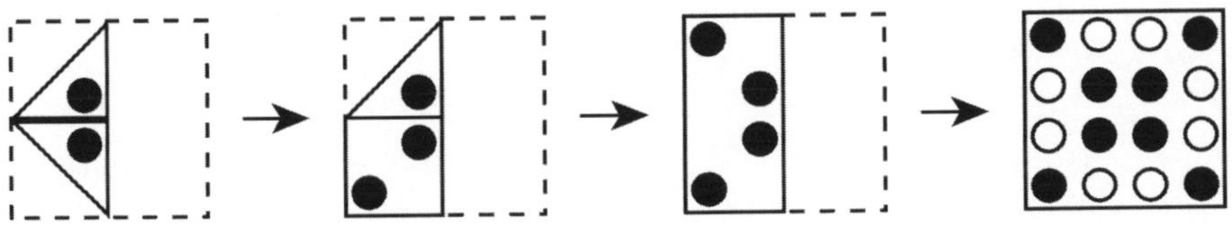

5. B:

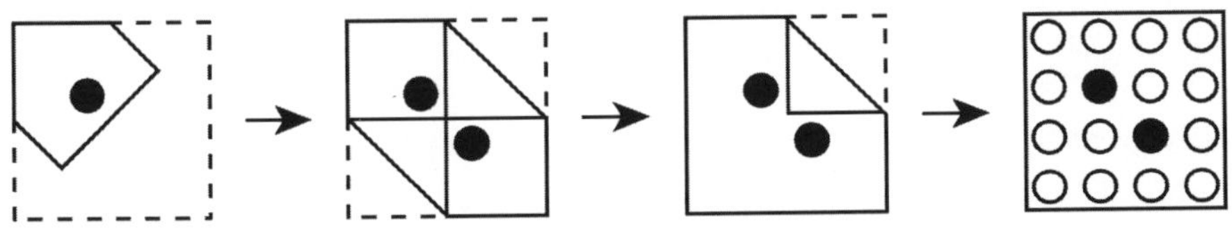

Written Comprehension

1. Beginning at 10:57 on the night of July 23rd, the 911 service received several phone calls reporting a large fight at a night club downtown. Four squad cars with eight officers responded immediately and found about a dozen adult males engaged in a melee. Within five minutes of arriving on the scene, they had the situation under control, and they began interviewing the combatants and witnesses. One of the combatants, Jose Mendez, told Officer Ronald Jones that the fight had begun when another man had assaulted his (Mendez's) date by tossing his drink in her face, and he had responded by punching the man. Officer Shantel Williams interviewed the man Mendez accused of starting the fight, Roland Hemphill, who denied tossing his drink on anyone, and said that he had tripped and accidentally spilled his drink on a woman, whose date then punched him. At this point, according to Hemphill and other witnesses, friends of both parties jumped in to defend their friends. Officer Mark Jones interviewed Tyreese Smith, the bartender, who said that he hadn't seen how it started as he had his back turned toward the crowd at the moment the fight erupted. Several other witnesses, who spoke to Officers Mike Smith and Wendell Brown, backed up Hemphill's account that the drink was spilled accidentally. There were no witnesses who claimed he tossed the drink deliberately. After interviewing nearly everyone on the scene, officers arrested Jose Mendez for battery.

Which officer interviewed the victim of Mendez's battery?

a. Officer Shantel Williams
b. Officer Ronald Jones
c. Officer Mike Smith
d. Officer Mark Jones

2. At approximately 2:44 p.m., Officer Rafael Sandoz located a stolen motor vehicle in a driveway of a residence in the 2000 block of Fair Havens Drive. The vehicle was unoccupied and it was quickly determined that it had recently been stolen from Orlando. Officer Sandoz called for backup. Shortly thereafter, Officers Macy Blevins and Officer Nick Glenn knocked on the door of the residence, and after identifying themselves and entering the house, questioned several individuals inside with regards to the stolen car. One of the individuals was in possession of suspected illegal narcotics and provided officers with false personal identifying information. She was eventually identified as Asia Campos and she was arrested on an outstanding warrant. While at the same location the three officers discovered another motor vehicle that had been reported stolen from Pensacola parked in the garage. They also discovered a motorcycle reported stolen from Pensacola behind the house. There were also illegal narcotics inside of the residence. The investigation led to the arrest of Ronald Holderman for the Orlando stolen motorcycle.

How many people were arrested?

a. One
b. Two
c. Three
d. Four

3. Just prior to Lights Out at a medium-security state prison, corrections staff staged an unannounced search for contraband after receiving several reports that at least two inmates possessed homemade knives and were planning to use them to "settle some scores." Although a thorough search turned up no knives, several contraband items were discovered and seized. Correctional Officer Steve Wilson found a marijuana cigarette in Inmate Reggie Wilson's pillow, and a cup of homemade wine in Inmate Robert Doolittle's cell. Correctional Officer Bob Jackson found a mobile phone in the cell of Inmates Mustafa Johnson and Dewayne Smith; both men denied that the phone was theirs. In a cell shared by Inmates Ryan McDonald and Brent Travers, Correctional Officer Emilio Padilla discovered three syringes and a metal spoon; both inmates claimed that the drug paraphernalia wasn't theirs and they were being "set up."

Altogether, how many contraband items were discovered?

a. Five
b. Six
c. Seven
d. Eight

4. On June 29 at approximately 11:30 a.m., two officers with from the police department's Southern Division were dispatched to a hotel in the 4500 block of Nevada Ave. to follow up on a missing person report about an adult, later identified as Eleanor Snowden, a 68-year-old female. The investigation revealed that Ms. Snowden registered as a guest of the hotel on June 20 but she has not been seen since June 22. Ms. Snowden has a condition that qualifies her as an at-risk member of the community and as such, our department is asking for assistance in locating her. Ms. Snowden is described as a white female, 5'08", 145 pounds, gray hair with blue eyes, and who was last seen wearing a gray hooded sweatshirt and blue pajama pants. A photograph of Ms. Snowden is available if requested.

How long has Ms. Snowden been missing?

a. Two days
b. Five days
c. Seven days
d. Ten days

5. Three officers responded to a call about a bank robbery in progress. When they got to the bank, the robbery was over and the criminals were gone. The head teller, Robin Benedict, told Officer Steve Atkins that four men in hoodies had pulled guns, ordered all customers to the floor, and demanded money. The bank's branch manager, Sheila Smith, told Officer Brenda Wilson that the robbers had been given four bags of cash, totaling a little over $20,000, and that tellers managed to get dye packs into three of the four bags. She estimated that one of the robbers was about 6 feet tall and about 180 pounds, one was 6 feet 3 inches and 225 pounds, another was probably around 5 feet 8 inches and 150 pounds, and the other was also about 5 feet 8 inches but weighed around 180 pounds. Each of them fled in a separate getaway vehicle—the tallest one took off going east in a brown van, the second tallest went west on a motorcycle, the short, stocky one fled west in a white Honda Civic, and the other shorter robber drove west in a small pickup truck. Each of the robbers took one bag of cash, but the branch manager wasn't sure which one had the bag without a dye pack.

What was the approximate height and weight of the robber who fled in a pickup truck?

a. 6 feet 0 inches and 180 lbs
b. 6 feet 3 inches and 225 lbs
c. 5 feet 8 inches and 150 lbs
d. 5 feet 8 inches and 180 lbs

6. During the early morning hours of January 22, patrol officers were dispatched to a residence on South Phelan Boulevard in reference to a felony menacing/shots fired call for service. During the questioning after they arrived on the scene, the officers were told by several witnesses that during a house party for a pay-for-view event, one of the guests, Donte Broomfield, 34 years of age, pulled a handgun. Witnesses stated that Mr. Broomfield threatened four women with the gun and physically assaulted two of them after they all rebuffed his advances. Witnesses further told the officers that Broomfield then left the party with his brother, and fired several rounds at the house as he was driven away by his brother. None of the rounds struck the house, but some of them did strike the vacant house next door. No one was injured during the shooting. Upon further investigation, officers discovered that Broomfield had allegedly pistol-whipped yet another acquaintance with a handgun at a different residence prior to the party. Officers attempted to locate the suspect through the night, but did not find him. It is believed he has fled the area.

How many people did Donte Broomfield assault at the pay-per-view party?

a. One
b. Two
c. Three
d. Four

7. The corrections supervisor handed out the schedule for the upcoming month. Corrections Officer Jones was assigned to Unit A for the first and third weeks, and Unit D for the second and fourth weeks. Corrections Officer Crews was assigned to Unit B for the first and third weeks, and Unit C for the second and fourth weeks. Corrections Officer Cantrell was assigned to Unit D for the first and third weeks, and Unit A for the second and fourth weeks. Corrections Officer Evers was assigned to Unit C for the first and third weeks, and Unit B for the second and fourth weeks. Corrections Officer Mason was assigned to Unit B for the first and third weeks, and Unit C for the second and fourth weeks. Corrections Officer Espinosa was assigned to Unit A for the first and third weeks, and Unit D for the second and fourth weeks. Corrections Officer Jefferson was assigned to Unit C for the first and third weeks, and Unit D for the second and fourth weeks. Corrections Officer Byers was assigned to Unit B for the first and third weeks, and Unit A for the second and fourth weeks.

Which corrections officers were assigned to Unit C for the second and fourth weeks of the month?

a. Cantrell and Jones
b. Crews and Mason
c. Byers and Cantrell
d. Evers and Jefferson

8. Officers Hollenbeck and Gerson were dispatched to a large department store to answer a call about shoplifting suspects in custody. When they arrived at the store, the customer service clerk directed them to the manager's office in the back. In the small office, they encountered the manager, an assistant manager, two security guards, and four suspects who were being detained. The four suspects identified themselves as Steve Nesmith, Brandon Jackson, Chad Pierson, and Ray Wellstone. All four were white males, and all were 18-19 years of age. A security guard told the officers that they had videotapes of all four suspects taking items and attempting to leave the store without paying. The manager then played the videotapes, which showed Nesmith putting on a hooded sweatshirt and removing the price tag, while Wellstone stuffed a dress down his pants. On another tape, Pierson is seen shoving several bags of candy into his pockets, and on the final tape, Jackson is seen filling his pockets with women's cosmetics. The four suspects admitted that they had taken the items, but told Officers Hollenbeck and Gerson that they were all students at a local university, and their actions were part of a hazing ritual, as they were all attempting to join a fraternity, which had ordered them to steal these items as a "prank." They insisted that they had planned to return and pay for the items after the hazing was over, and asked for leniency because none of them had any prior arrests. The officers arrested all four for shoplifting and then had them transported downtown for processing.

Who stole an item of women's clothing?

a. Nesmith
b. Jackson
c. Pierson
d. Wellstone

9. Officers Regina Petty and Thomas Fritz responded to a call about a loud party in progress at 5792 Windmere Avenue. Arriving at the house at approximately 1:30 AM, they heard loud rap music blaring from the house as soon as they exited their car. A couple dozen people were outside the house, spread out in the yard, on the porch, and on the sidewalk. As they approached the house, a man came out of the house next door and stopped the officers. He said "these people have been nothing but trouble since they moved in a year ago", and it was high time the police cracked down on them. According to the neighbor, within the last six months, police officers had been to the house to investigate public intoxication, another time for a domestic dispute call, a few weeks later for loud music, then again for cars parking illegally and impeding traffic, and the last time for a person who was drunk and disorderly. The officers said they were aware of the recent history of the occupants, and asked the neighbor to go back inside his house. They then approached the party house and asked for the homeowner. When he came to the door, the officers told him to end the party and send everyone home, or everyone there would be charged with disturbing the peace. The homeowner briefly argued with the officers, but then complied with their instructions.

According to the neighbor, how many times had the police been to the house in the last six months?

a. Five
b. Six
c. Seven
d. Eight

10. Police are searching for a driver who fled from a car after a chase by several officers Tuesday night. At 9:21 p.m., Officer James Logan attempted to stop a vehicle for speeding on Grosvenor Drive. According to Officer Logan, the driver failed to yield and sped off, heading south on Grosvenor, then turning east onto Eldridge Avenue. After nearly causing a collision with another car at the intersection of Scranton Street, he turned north onto Huddleston Pike and appeared to be heading for the freeway. He managed to elude the pursuing officers for only a short time, however, as he lost control of the car when he tried to cut through a parking lot and one of the tires blew out after jumping the curb. The driver fled the scene on foot and has not yet been caught, but he has been identified, according to the report. It was soon discovered that the vehicle had been stolen at approximately 9:15 p.m.

Where did the driver nearly collide with another car?

a. The onramp of the freeway
b. Cutting through a parking lot
c. The intersection of Grosvenor and Eldridge
d. The intersection of Eldridge and Scranton

11. At approximately 7:00 p.m., Officer John Ramirez and Officer Bettina Woolsey were dispatched to a report of a fight taking place in the 1500 block of Maple Avenue. The caller stated that the males in the house had begun arguing over a football game on TV, which led to a physical altercation, and that one of her sons was unconscious and her nephew was bleeding. When the officers arrived, the woman answered the door and let them in the house, where they found four males who had obviously been fighting. Steven Jones, the woman's husband and the owner of the house, had a torn shirt and a lump on his forehead. His brother, Eric Jones, looked disheveled but didn't have any obvious injuries. Both men appeared to be between 40 and 50 years of age. Mark Jones, the son of Steven Jones and the female caller, and an occupant of the house, was lying on the couch and appeared to be woozy. Ethan Jones, the son of Eric Jones, had a makeshift bandage around his head, which was stained with blood. These two men were in their early twenties. None of the men were very cooperative with the officers. The female who called police said that her son and his cousin were watching a football game when her husband and brother-in-law demanded that they change the station so they could watch a different game. The younger men refused, and that's what started the fight. She said alcohol was also a factor. However, all of the men denied that they needed medical help, and they all refused to press charges, so the officers gave them a stern warning and departed without making any arrests.

Who had a bloody forehead?

a. Eric Jones
b. Steven Jones
c. Mark Jones
d. Ethan Jones

12. After a series of mass brawls in the TV room of the main unit, prison officials decided to crack down on known or suspected members of prison gangs, by moving them to another unit, or transferring them to another prison. Six members of the Latin Kings were moved to other units, while three were transferred. Four members of the Outlaws were moved to other units, while two were transferred. Four members of the Gangster Disciples were moved to other units, while six were transferred. Seven members of the Mexican Mafia were moved to other units, while two were transferred. After these changes, violence in the main unit decreased substantially, while violence in the other units did not increase.

Which prison gang saw the most members moved out of the unit or transferred?

a. Mexican Mafia
b. Outlaws
c. Gangster Disciples
d. Latin Kings

13. At approximately 9:30 p.m. on Wednesday, several officers were dispatched to the Bent Tree Gardens apartment complex at the intersection of Bent Tree Road and 14th Avenue, in response to calls about a large group of people fighting. Callers said the group had been arguing and screaming at each other for nearly two hours, and were on the verge of brawling. Upon arrival from a side alley, officers counted ten men and eight women in the brightly lit parking lot, divided into two groups facing each other, and heard many of them exchanging threats of violence. When the crowd realized police had arrived, they took off running in various directions. All escaped except for two women, who were arrested and transported downtown for processing. Shortly after midnight, 911 callers reported that the group was back in the parking lot, again disturbing the peace and threatening to fight. This time, a larger number of officers responded, and while many of the brawlers successfully fled on foot, officers were able to detain five men and three women. One of the men and two of the women were determined to be bystanders, and let go, but the rest were arrested and taken in for booking.

How many women were arrested?

a. One
b. Two
c. Three
d. Four

14. On Tuesday, 09/22, at approximately 4:11 a.m., a call for service was received about a rollover car accident in the area of Greenhills Blvd. and Robertson Rd. When they arrived on the scene, officers located a single vehicle on the sidewalk on the south side of the eastbound lanes of Greenhills Blvd., just west of Robertson Rd. That vehicle, a Toyota Corolla, had left the roadway and rolled over, landing on its roof, ejecting two female occupants and trapping two additional male occupants. All occupants were transported by ambulance to area hospitals. The driver, who was identified as 26-year-old Caitlyn Malcolm, was evaluated and arrested for DUI and Vehicular Assault. The 22-year-old female passenger, Britney Maddox, is currently being treated for serious injuries. The 26-year-old and 29-year-old male passengers, Ryan Tellinger and Rob Tellinger, were treated for less serious injuries and discharged from the hospital. The eastbound lanes of Greenhills Blvd. were temporarily closed to facilitate the investigation. The Major Accidents Unit responded to conduct the investigation in conjunction with the originally responding patrol officers.

Who was charged with Vehicular Assault?

a. Britney Maddox
b. Caitlyn Malcolm
c. Rob Tellinger
d. Ryan Tellinger

15. After a recent surge of violent crimes in a local neighborhood, gang activity suppression officers were out in force last weekend, and made several arrests. On Friday night, they made three arrests for selling drugs, five for loitering, six for public intoxication, and nine for outstanding warrants. On Saturday afternoon, they made two arrests for selling drugs, nine for loitering, and five for outstanding warrants. On Saturday night and into early Sunday morning, they arrested fifteen people for outstanding warrants, seven for selling drugs, ten for loitering, and six for public intoxication. Police officials said the crackdown will continue until the neighborhood sees a significant reduction in the crime rate.

Altogether, how many people were arrested for selling drugs during the crackdown?

a. Three
b. Six
c. Nine
d. Twelve

Written Expression

1. The depudy talked to the sheriff about possibly going back to school and earning a bachelor's degree.

One word in the above sentence is misspelled. It is:

a. depudy
b. sheriff
c. possibly
d. bachelor's

2. The witness ________ the suspect as a man in his late twenties.

Which of these words would be the correct choice to fill in the blank?

a. subscribed
b. prescribed
c. described
d. ascribed

3. The prison transport van arived over two hours late, requiring the officers to have to fill out overtime authorization forms.

One word in the above sentence is misspelled. It is:

a. transport
b. arived
c. requiring
d. authorization

4. If you will have to miss work due to illness, you ________ notify the department no later than two hours before your shift starts.

Which of these words or phrases would be the correct choice to fill in the blank?

a. are
b. have
c. must
d. must have

5. The robbery took place in broad daylight, shocking many of the small town's cittizens.

One word in the above sentence is misspelled. It is:

a. robbery
b. broad
c. shocking
d. cittizens

6. NOTICE: It ____ not permitted to carry a concealed weapon on these premises.

Which of these words would be the correct choice to fill in the blank?

a. is
b. am
c. isn't
d. are

7. The funural procession for the mayor consisted of over one hundred vehicles.

One word in the above sentence is misspelled. It is:

a. funural
b. procession
c. consisted
d. vehicles

8. At roll call, everyone will be _____ his or her rounds for the day.

Which of these words or phrases would be the correct choice to fill in the blank?

a. have assigned
b. assigned
c. requested
d. required

9. The weather report brought unpleasent news—there's a possibility of a tornado.

One word in the above sentence is misspelled. It is:

a. weather
b. unpleasent
c. possibility
d. tornado

10. The best policy is to always ____ prepared for the worst.

Which of these words or phrases would be the correct choice to fill in the blank?

a. been
b. to be
c. are being
d. be

11. The sergeant will summarize his findings for the cheif, who will prepare a report for the mayor.

One word in the above sentence is misspelled. It is:

a. sergeant
b. summarize
c. cheif
d. mayor

12. No one will ______ the academy without first passing a background check.

Which of these words or phrases would be the correct choice to fill in the blank?

a. allowed to
b. admitted to
c. be allowed to
d. be admitted to

13. The outgoing union president said the membership would pay a steap price for voting him out.

One word in the above sentence is misspelled. It is:

a. outgoing
b. membership
c. steap
d. voting

14. The police spokesman said extra patrols ______ added downtown due to the number of robberies going up 25% in six months.

Which of these words or phrases would be the correct choice to fill in the blank?

a. have been
b. has been
c. have
d. been

15. The corrections officer orientation manual states clearly that officers are not allowed to endorce any politician or attend any political functions while in uniform.

One word in the above sentence is misspelled. It is:

a. orientation
b. manual
c. endorce
d. functions

Memorization

This section contains several photographs. Study each picture for two minutes. Then turn the page and answer some questions about the picture.

Photo 1

1. How many people appear in this photo?

a. 12
b. 13
c. 14
d. 15

2. How many people in the first row are wearing a dress?

a. 0
b. 1
c. 2
d. 3

Photo 2

3. Of the three people in the main area of the picture, how many are wearing glasses?

a. 0
b. 1
c. 2
d. 3

4. What is the woman whose luggage the dog is sniffing doing?

a. Taking a nap
b. Looking at her phone
c. Talking to a police officer
d. Reading a book

Photo 3

5. Which officer is taller?

a. Both officers are the same height
b. It's impossible to tell from the picture
c. The officer on the left
d. The officer on the right.

6. Which officer is wearing sunglasses?

a. Neither one
b. Both
c. The officer on the left
d. The officer on the right

7. Which officer is in short sleeves?

a. Neither one
b. Both
c. The officer on the left
d. The officer on the right

8. Which officer is wearing a cap?

a. Neither one
b. Both
c. The officer on the left
d. The officer on the right

9. Which officer is wearing gloves?

a. Neither one
b. Both
c. The officer on the left
d. The officer on the right

Photo 4

10. Which officer is tallest?

a. The officer on the left
b. The officer in the middle
c. The officer on the right
d. They are all about the same height

11. Which officer is holding his beverage in his right hand?

a. The officer on the left
b. The officer in the middle
c. The officer on the right
d. All of them

12. What does the street sign say?

a. 42nd St
b. 42nd Ave
c. 24th St
d. 24th Ave

Photo 5

13. According to the mileage sign, how far away is Condon?

a. 38 miles
b. 138 miles
c. 159 miles
d. 59 miles

14. Which sign is taller?

a. The mileage sign
b. The road sign
c. Both signs are the same height
d. It's impossible to tell from the picture

15. In which direction is the arrow on the road sign pointing?

a. Right
b. Left
c. Up
d. Down

Problem Sensitivity

1. During a power outage across the city, your department has started receiving sporadic complaints about looting. As you patrol the area near dusk, which of these people should you be most suspicious of?

a. A man sitting on a porch bobbing his head to music while wearing what appear to be new, expensive headphones
b. A man pulling a kid's wagon down the sidewalk containing four cases of beer
c. A teenager walking down the street wearing the latest in urban fashion
d. A man in bike shorts and shoes sitting on a curb drinking from a water bottle next to a very expensive racing bicycle

2. While patrolling your beat around midnight, you see three teenage males near the entrance of an athletic shoe store in a strip mall. Pulling over, you ask them what they're up to. At first, they say they're just "hanging out." When they see that you're skeptical of the story, one of them says that they thought maybe the store was still open. About the same time, another one says that they're waiting to be first in line when the store opens in the morning because a popular sneaker company is releasing a new shoe. What is most likely going on?

a. They were just hanging out
b. They thought the store was open but were mistaken
c. They want to be first in line when the store opens in the morning
d. They were planning on breaking into the store

3. Which behavior by a driver you just happen to have been following for a while should most concern you?

a. The driver begins constantly changing lanes, using his signal for each lane change
b. The driver appears to be singing at the top of his voice
c. The driver signals for a right turn, but then turns his signal off and proceeds straight
d. The driver rolls down his window at every stop and lets his arm hang out the window

4. You and your partner are responding to a call from a homeowner who says his car was broken into, and several items are missing. On your way to the residence, you pass another house where two adult males are in the yard, in boxing stances, shouting threats at each other in what sounds like a dispute over a female. What should you do?

a. Proceed to the first call and request dispatch to send someone to the dispute
b. Ask the dispatcher what you should do
c. Stop and deal with the situation and notify dispatch about the unplanned stop
d. Ignore it because responding to the car break-in is your top priority

5. At a departmental meeting, the new corrections supervisor, whom you've never worked under before, outlines some new rules about conducting cell searches for contraband. You are near the back and the supervisor is soft-spoken, and you didn't make out everything he said. What should you do?

a. Talk to some fellow officers later to find out exactly what the supervisor said
b. Assume that the new rules are not much different than the old rules and don't worry
c. After the meeting, ask the supervisor to clarify what you didn't understand
d. Don't worry about it, because if it's important, it will be in a departmental email

6. Your law enforcement agency is on heightened alert after a terrorist attack in a European city. While you are detailed to a parade for the Fourth of July, some concerned parade spectators approach you and tell you that a backpack appears to have been abandoned about by a lamppost about a block away. It's been there for over two hours, and they are afraid it contains a bomb. You walk down to look at it, and its appearance tells you nothing. It's simply a backpack, that appears to be full, that has been sitting unattended for at least two hours. What should you do?

a. Order everyone out of the area and call for the bomb squad
b. Tell them someone probably forgot it and if it's still there in two hours you'll notify your superiors
c. Poke it with your baton or a stick to see if it feels suspicious
d. Open it to see what's inside

7. Your turn on your lights after seeing that the plates on the car in front of you have been expired for three months. The driver, who doesn't appear to be under the influence of alcohol, gets out of the car with wallet in hand and begins walking toward you. When you order him back into the car, he says he's in a hurry and "would rather just get it over with." When you again order him back into his car, he takes out a hundred dollar bill and offers it to you if you forget this ever happened and let him go on his way. What is the most likely reason the man is refusing to follow your orders and offering you a bribe?

a. The driver is on drugs
b. The car is stolen
c. The driver is in a hurry to get somewhere
d. There is something in the car the driver doesn't want you to see

8. In front of a convenience store, while in an unmarked car, you see a boy of about 11 or 12 years of age approach a man who's entering the store. The two talk briefly, and the boy appears to hand the man something, and the man then enters the store. A few minutes later, the man emerges from the store with a brown paper bag. He approaches the boy, reaches into the bag, and takes a small item out and hands it to the boy, who shoves it in his pocket. What is the most likely explanation of this scenario?

a. The boy loaned the man some money and the man is giving him some change
b. The man bought a pack of cigarettes for the boy who is too young to buy them legally
c. The man bought gum for the boy who had to wait outside for his mother
d. The boy found a winning lotto ticket but is too young to cash it so the man cashed it for him

9. On patrol, you turn down a street and discover that a terrible collision has just taken place at the next intersection. There are at least four people outside of the cars with what appear to be serious injuries, and there are other injured people still in the two vehicles. After informing dispatch that several ambulances will probably be required, you get out to offer assistance. Which accident victim should you attempt to help first?

a. A female teenager who is moaning and barely conscious
b. An elderly woman who is walking around and appears disoriented
c. A young adult woman who is bleeding profusely from her left arm
d. A young boy on the ground who is crying and says his arm is broken

10. A woman flags you down near a public park. She directs you to a park bench, where an elderly man is sitting, surrounded by a few concerned joggers and walkers. He is sweating profusely and disoriented, and is slurring his speech. What is the most likely explanation for his condition?

a. He is under the influence of illegal drugs
b. He has been mugged in the park
c. He is suffering from Alzheimer's disease
d. He is experiencing a medical emergency

11. While you are driving in your cruiser on a busy city four-lane road, with a speed limit of 45 MPH, you are passed by a car in the left lane going at least 60 MPH. As soon as the car passes you, its brake lights come on and it slows to around 40 MPH. As you turn on your lights to pull the car over for speeding, someone throws a small object out the front passenger window, and the car accelerates instead of pulling over. What is the most likely explanation for this?

a. The driver didn't see your flashing lights and doesn't know you want him to pull over
b. The driver and passenger are involved in illegal drug use or sales and fear arrest
c. There is a medical emergency and the driver needs an escort to the hospital
d. The driver is looking for a safer place to pull over, like a side street

12. You are working on desk duty, and you receive a call about an abandoned vehicle, a late model pickup truck. The caller says it has been parked in front of her house for over a week without moving. Upon running the license plate number through the computer system, you learn that the plates are registered to a completely different vehicle, an older sedan. What is the most likely explanation for this?

a. The truck is stolen
b. There was a mix-up at the DMV and the wrong plates got issued
c. The same person owns both vehicles and put the wrong plates on the truck
d. The caller is mistaken about what kind of vehicle it is

13. On foot patrol on a busy street, you overhear the four discussions below. Which of these should most concern you?

a. Two women quietly discussing the weather on a bench
b. Two men arguing loudly about which NFL team has better prospects
c. Two women loudly discussing religion as they walk down the street
d. Two men shouting at each other from their cars over the right to a parking space

14. You are called to the scene of an assault and robbery downtown. An elderly woman was walking on the sidewalk when an assailant walked up, punched her, and took her purse. After the ambulance transports the victim to the hospital, you interview four witnesses who say they saw attack take place. Here are their descriptions of the perpetrator:

> #1. "It was a black kid, probably 18 or 20. He walks up and punches her in the face and takes her purse. He was probably about 5" 8" tall and I guess around 150 lbs. He had on a dark blue hoodie."
>
> #2. "It was a white guy. He grabbed her purse and then pushed her down and took off running. He was wearing blue jeans and a white t-shirt. About 6 feet tall and 200 pounds."
>
> #3. "I didn't get a good look at him, so I don't know if he was white, black, or whatever. Or how old he was. But as fast as he moved, I'd guess early twenties. He was probably about 5' 10" or so and around 165 pounds. He had on a dark gray hoodie. He knocked her down and took her purse.
>
> #4. "I think he was Hispanic. Or maybe a light skinned black guy. About 5' 9" or so and I would guess 160 pounds. Wearing a black hoodie. Runs up and slugs the old lady and takes her purse."

Which of these people most likely didn't actually witness the attack?

a. 1
b. 2
c. 3
d. 4

15. Your patrol area has been getting a lot of rain lately, and there is a flood warning in effect. While you're on patrol on a Sunday, another torrential downpour begins, and because of the previous amounts of rain, roads begin to flood. Several roads will need to be blocked with patrol cars to prevent cars from being caught in the flood. Which of these roads should be the highest priority for blocking with your patrol car?

a. A two-lane road that's mainly used as an entrance to a huge industrial park
b. A six lane main thoroughfare through the middle of town
c. A busy two-lane side road where several drivers and passengers have drowned in past floods
d. A cul-de-sac in a neighborhood that tends to flood

Number Facility

1. 236

+301

a. 505
b. 507
c. 535
d. 537

2. 356

- 167

a. 189
b. 198
c. 211
d. 298

3. 5,306

-3,487

a. 1,181
b. 1,819
c. 2,119
d. 2,189

4. $7\overline{)917}$

a. 131
b. 131 R4
c. 145
d. 145 R4

5. $\frac{38}{100}$ **as a decimal**

a. 0.38
b. 0.038
c. 3.8
d. 0.0038

6.

6.8

11.3

+ 0.06

a. 17.16
b. 17.70
c. 18.16
d. 18.70

7. 0.58 - 0.39=

a. 0.19
b. 1.9
c. 0.29
d. 2.9

8. Solve: 0.25 × 0.03 =

a. 75
b. 0.075
c. 0.75
d. 0.0075

9. $\mathbf{3\frac{1}{8} + 6 + \frac{3}{7} =}$

a. $9\frac{31}{56}$
b. $9\frac{1}{2}$
c. $9\frac{21}{56}$
d. $9\frac{7}{8}$

10. $\mathbf{1\frac{1}{4} \times 3\frac{2}{5} \times 1\frac{2}{3} =}$

a. $7\frac{1}{12}$
b. $5\frac{5}{6}$
c. $6\frac{7}{12}$
d. $8\frac{11}{15}$

11. Thirty-six hundredths as a percent.

a. 36%
b. 0.36%
c. 0.036%
d. 3.6%

12. 40% of 900

a. 280
b. 340
c. 360
d. 420

13. 6% of 25

a. .3
b. 1.5
c. 3.0
d. 15

14. Ratio of 4 to 16 = (?)%

a. 2
b. 4
c. 12
d. 25

15. 37% as a decimal

a. .0037
b. .037
c. .37
d. 3.7

Mathematical Reasoning

1. Mr. Thompson fills his 25.2 gallon gasoline tank with gas that costs $2.98 a gallon. Which is the best approximation of the cost of the gasoline?

a. $50
b. $60
c. $75
d. $90

2. A wealthy uncle decides to give away half of his fortune. Each of his 5 relatives is to receive an equal share. Which of the statements below describes how this can be done?

a. Multiply his wealth by 1/5 and give this amount to each of his relatives
b. Multiply his wealth by 1/2 and give this amount to each of his relatives
c. Multiply his wealth by 1/10 and give this amount to each of his relatives
d. Multiply his wealth by 2/5 and give this amount to each of his relatives

3. Jasper collects 1,082 cans of food. He gives a certain number of cans to the first local charity he finds. He now has 602 cans of food. How many cans of food did he give to the first local charity?

a. 430
b. 480
c. 682
d. 1,684

4. Hannah ran 12 laps every day for 8 days. How many laps did she run in all?

a. 108
b. 96
c. 84
d. 72

5. Kevin approved 13 trees out of every group of trees he surveyed. He surveyed 15 groups of trees. How many trees did he approve?

a. 155
b. 165
c. 195
d. 205

6. Three friends sold cupcakes for a fundraiser. Eli sold 84 cupcakes, John sold 46 cupcakes, and Kim sold 72 cupcakes. Which of the following is the best estimate for the number of cupcakes the three friends sold in all?

a. 180
b. 200
c. 210
d. 190

7. Lynn has $316 to spend on groceries for the month. He plans to spend the same amount of money on groceries each week. Which of the following is the best estimate for the amount of money he can spend on groceries each week?

a. $65
b. $75
c. $90
d. $95

8. Carlisle charges $21.95 per hair cut and has completed 30 haircuts this week. Which of the following is the best approximation for the total charges for all haircuts?

a. $450
b. $600
c. $750
d. $800

9. Which of the following is the most reasonable estimate for the length of a book?

a. $\frac{1}{2}$ meter
b. $11\frac{1}{2}$ inches
c. 8 millimeters
d. 2 yards

10. Which of the following is the most reasonable estimate for the weight of a chair?

a. 1 ton
b. 15 pounds
c. 3 kilograms
d. 6 grams

11. Toasty Donut Shop makes 141 donuts one morning. The donuts are packaged in boxes of 12 for delivery. How many single donuts are left over?

a. 3
b. 9
c. 6
d. 1

12. A square flower garden has an area of 81 feet. What is the length of one side of the garden?

a. 9 feet
b. 20.25 feet
c. 40.5 feet
d. 324 feet

13. Jodi made a sum of money yesterday at a bake sale. She spent half of the money to buy more ingredients for next week's bake sale, and then spent $12 to go to the movies. Jodi has $17 remaining. How much did she make yesterday at the bake sale?

a. $36
b. $58
c. $46
d. $41

14. A little boy decides to give away all of his marbles. Each of his 4 friends is to receive an equal share. Which of the statements below describes how this can be done?

a. Multiply his marbles by 4 and give this amount to each of his friends
b. Multiply his marbles by 2 and give this amount to each of his friends
c. Multiply his marbles by 1/2 and give this amount to each of his friends
d. Multiply his marbles by 1/4 and give this amount to each of his friends

15. A grocery store determines the price of a gallon milk, *P*, in dollars will be determined by multiplying the wholesale price, *W*, in dollars by 1.5 and adding 25 cents. Which expression below represents this relationship?

a. $P = 1.5 + W + 0.25$
b. $P = 0.25W + 1.5$
c. $P = 1.75W$
d. $P = 1.5W + 0.25$

16. Mr. Aguilera needs 71 feet of fencing that costs $3.98 per foot. Which is the best approximation for the price of the fencing?

a. $210
b. $240
c. $320
d. $280

17. William is going to work out of the country for a total of 145 days. Expressed in weeks and days, how long will William be gone?

a. 24 weeks and 1 day
b. 20 weeks and 5 days
c. 29 weeks
d. 21 weeks and 2 days

Deductive Reasoning

1. Money Laundering

(a) A person commits an offense if the person knowingly:

(1) acquires or maintains an interest in, conceals, possesses, transfers, or transports the proceeds of criminal activity;

(2) conducts, supervises, or facilitates a transaction involving the proceeds of criminal activity;

(3) invests, expends, or receives, or offers to invest, expend, or receive, the proceeds of criminal activity or funds that the person believes are the proceeds of criminal activity; or

(4) finances or invests or intends to finance or invest funds that the person believes are intended to further the commission of criminal activity.

(a-1) Knowledge of the specific nature of the criminal activity giving rise to the proceeds is not required to establish a culpable mental state under this section.

(b) It is a defense to prosecution under this section that the person acted with intent to facilitate the lawful seizure, forfeiture, or disposition of funds or other legitimate law enforcement purpose pursuant to the laws of this state or the US

(c) It is a defense to prosecution under this section that the transaction was necessary to preserve a person's right to representation as guaranteed by the Sixth Amendment of the United States Constitution and by Article 1, Section 10, of the Texas Constitution or that the funds were received as bona fide legal fees by a licensed attorney and at the time of their receipt, the attorney did not have actual knowledge that the funds were derived from criminal activity.

(d) An offense under this section is:

(1) a state jail felony if the value of the funds is $2,500 or more but less than $30,000;

(2) a felony of the third degree if the value of the funds is $30,000 or more but less than $150,000;

(3) a felony of the second degree if the value of the funds is $150,000 or more but less than $300,000; or

(4) a felony of the first degree if the value of the funds is $300,000 or more.

A woman suspects her husband has started selling drugs out of their rural home while she works during the day. When she finds $38,000 in cash hidden in a closet, she is convinced of it. Wanting no part of the illicit operation, and fearing arrest, one day while her husband is away, she puts the cash in the trunk of her car and begins driving to the county sheriff's office nearly ten miles away. On her way there, a state trooper pulls her over for speeding, and when he discovers the cash, arrests her for suspicious activity. Based on the information above, what level of felony is the woman likely to be convicted of?

a. First degree felony
b. Second degree felony
c. Third degree felony
d. She will not be convicted

2. Here are some rules from the Police Officer Manual for a large city. Breaking any of these rules can result in receiving disciplinary action, up to and including being fired:

Rule 25: Failure to inventory and process recovered property in conformance with department orders.

Rule 27: Disseminating, releasing, altering, defacing or removing any department record or information concerning police matters except as provided by department orders.

Rule 28: Participating in any partisan political campaign or activity.

Rule 29: Associating or fraternizing with any person known to have been convicted of any felony or misdemeanor, either State or Federal, excluding traffic and municipal ordinance violations.

Rule 30: Discussing bail with a person who is in custody except by those specifically authorized to let to bond.

Rule 32: Giving an opinion as to fine or penalty.

Rule 34: Recommending any professional or commercial service.

Rule 37: Advising any person engaged in a professional or commercial service that such professional or commercial services may be needed.

Rule 41: Soliciting or accepting any gratuity, or soliciting or accepting a gift, present, reward, or other thing of value for any service rendered as a department member, or as a condition for the rendering of such service, or as a condition for not performing sworn duties.

You are a police officer who has sworn to follow the above rules. You're also a member of a neighborhood softball team, which you have played on for several years. At the first meeting for the upcoming season, you learn that a new member of the team is a convicted felon. He was released from prison five years ago after being sentenced for grand theft auto. However, he has not been in any trouble with the law in the five years since his parole, has a respectable job, and has started a family. Based on the above information, what should you do?

a. Nothing, as the man is no longer a criminal
b. Associate with him at games, but not anywhere else
c. Quit the team immediately
d. Talk the situation over with your immediate supervisor

3. From the Florida Administrative Code:

(1) When any employee or person supervising inmates witnesses an act or has reason to believe that an act has been committed by an inmate which is in violation of the rules or procedures of the Department and that employee determines that the infraction can be properly disposed of without a formal disciplinary report, the employee shall take the necessary action to resolve the matter.

(2) If the employee cannot resolve the matter through a verbal reprimand or corrective consultation, the employee shall consult with and obtain approval from his or her supervisor regarding preparation of a formal disciplinary report, unless the employee is at the department head level or correctional officer lieutenant level or above.

(3) When it appears that laws of the state have been violated, the Office of the Inspector General shall be notified, who will, in turn, contact the State Attorney when deemed appropriate. If the State Attorney decides to prosecute, his office shall be consulted as to the suitability of disciplinary action being taken by the institution prior to the prosecution being concluded.

(4) The commission of acts that should normally result in consideration for formal disciplinary action shall not be subject to such action when these acts are directly associated with an inmate's intentional self-injurious behavior.

According to the above information, which of these situations would not result in an inmate being punished?

a. An inmate smoking a cigarette in a no-smoking area
b. An inmate burning his arm with a lit cigarette
c. An inmate smoking marijuana
d. An inmate possessing a cell phone

4. From the Florida Administrative Code:

(1) The following grooming standards shall apply to all Department of Corrections employees, including all non-uniformed employees and contracted employees, while performing official duties:

(a) All employees shall maintain a professional appearance at all times while performing official duties.

(b) All employees shall maintain personal hygiene and shall keep themselves personally neat and clean while on duty.

(c) Clothing will be clean and pressed as is appropriate for the particular garment.

(d) Clothing shall be appropriate for the particular assignment.

(e) Shoes will be clean, presentable, and appropriate for the particular assignment.

(f) Policies regarding the wearing of neck ties for office staff will be determined by the Secretary, Deputy Secretary and Office Directors.

(g) Hair will be neat, clean, trimmed and present a groomed appearance. If the hair is dyed, only natural shades will be permitted.

(h) Earrings are prohibited for male staff. Earrings for female staff will constitute the only body piercing ornaments allowed. No employee will display while on duty any other jewelry of which any part has been pierced into or through the skin or flesh of any part of the body.

(i) Undergarments shall not be visible.

(j) All employees shall dress in a manner appropriate to their positions and duties and shall avoid eccentricities in their personal appearance.

(k) All employees shall dress in a manner required by the court for all court appearances.

A female corrections officer shows up for work one day wearing earrings and with blue frosted highlights in her hair. Which of the above would she be violating?

a. (f)
b. (g)
c. (h)
d. (j)

5. From the Florida Administrative Code:

(1) Only five approved visitors, 12 years of age or older, at any time, may visit an inmate in the visiting area. Children 11 years old and younger do not count against the five approved visitors.

(2) A visitor's initial check-in shall take place in a location that minimizes weather exposure and provides restrooms.

(3) Visitors shall be required to register for visiting through the automated visiting record. The failure to do so or providing false information shall result in denial or termination of the visit and suspension of visiting privileges.

(4) All visitors sixteen years of age or older must present a valid form of picture identification for visiting registration. Acceptable forms of identification are identification cards that contain a photograph, current address, and date of birth and physical characteristics of the individual. Signatures are not required if the identification otherwise complies with all other standards of proper identification.

(5) A visitor seventeen years old or younger who cannot furnish proof of emancipation must be accompanied during a visit by an approved parent, legal guardian, or authorized adult and must remain under the supervision of that adult at all times, to include when the minor is subject to being searched under the provisions of Rule 33-601.726, F.A.C. An authorized non-parental adult accompanying a visiting minor must provide a notarized document of guardianship from the minor's parent or legal guardian (neither of which may be an inmate except as provided below) granting permission for the minor to visit a specifically identified inmate. The document shall be notarized by someone other than the non-parental adult accompanying the minor and shall be updated every six months from the date of issue. In cases where it can be determined that legal custody remains with the incarcerated parent or legal guardian and has not been given to another adult by the court, a notarized statement from the incarcerated parent or guardian shall be acceptable for purposes of authorizing children of the inmate to visit. Any such authorization remains subject to any relevant court orders or relevant departmental rules regarding the inmate's contact with the minor in question. Falsification of a document of guardianship shall result in the person being subject to suspension of visiting privileges pursuant to paragraph 33-601.731(9)(d), F.A.C.

According to the above, which children need to register through the automated visiting record?

a. All children
b. Children eleven years of age or older
c. Children twelve years of age or older
d. Children sixteen years of age or older

6. Sale or possession of illegal fireworks:

(4)(a) "Fireworks" means and includes any combustible or explosive composition or substance or combination of substances or, except as hereinafter provided, any article prepared for the purpose of producing a visible or audible effect by combustion, explosion, deflagration, or detonation. The term includes blank cartridges and toy cannons in which explosives are used, the type of balloons which require fire underneath to propel them, firecrackers, torpedoes, skyrockets, roman candles, dago bombs, and any fireworks containing any explosives or flammable compound or any tablets or other device containing any explosive substance.

(b) "Fireworks" does not include sparklers approved by the division pursuant to s. 791.013; toy pistols, toy canes, toy guns, or other devices in which paper caps containing twenty-five hundredths grains or less of explosive compound are used, providing they are so constructed that the hand cannot come in contact with the cap when in place for the explosion; and toy pistol paper caps which contain less than twenty hundredths grains of explosive mixture, the sale and use of which shall be permitted at all times.

(c) "Fireworks" also does not include the following novelties and trick noisemakers:

1. A snake or glow worm, which is a pressed pellet of not more than 10 grams of pyrotechnic composition that produces a large, snakelike ash which expands in length as the pellet burns and that does not contain mercuric thiocyanate.

2. A smoke device, which is a tube or sphere containing not more than 10 grams of pyrotechnic composition that, upon burning, produces white or colored smoke as the primary effect.

3. A trick noisemaker, which is a device that produces a small report intended to surprise the user and which includes:

a. A party popper, which is a small plastic or paper device containing not more than 16 milligrams of explosive composition that is friction sensitive, which is ignited by pulling a string protruding from the device, and which expels a paper streamer and produces a small report.
b. A booby trap, which is a small tube with a string protruding from both ends containing not more than 16 milligrams of explosive compound, which is ignited by pulling the ends of the string, and which produces a small report.
c. A snapper, which is a small, paper-wrapped device containing not more than four milligrams of explosive composition coated on small bits of sand, and which, when dropped, explodes, producing a small report. A snapper may not contain more than 250 milligrams of total sand and explosive composition.
d. A trick match, which is a kitchen or book match which is coated with not more than 16 milligrams of explosive or pyrotechnic composition and which, upon ignition, produces a small report or shower of sparks.

Which of the following falls under the definition of illegal fireworks?

a. Trick match
b. Party popper
c. Toy gun
d. Roman candle

7. Abuse, aggravated abuse, and neglect of a child; penalties.

(a) A person who willfully or by culpable negligence neglects a child and in so doing causes great bodily harm, permanent disability, or permanent disfigurement to the child commits a felony of the second degree.

(b) A person who knowingly or willfully abuses a child without causing great bodily harm, permanent disability, or permanent disfigurement to the child commits a felony of the third degree.

(c) A person who willfully or by culpable negligence neglects a child without causing great bodily harm, permanent disability, or permanent disfigurement to the child commits a felony of the third degree.

You have been dispatched to a house because neighbors called the police saying the woman who lives there lets her six year old and eight year old children play in the street long after it gets dark. When you arrive at 10:15 pm, the children are indeed playing in the street, but appear to be healthy and have no injuries. You arrest the woman for her actions. According to the above what kind of crime has she committed?

a. Misdemeanor
b. Third-degree felony
c. Second-degree felony
d. First-degree felony

8. Gang-related offenses; enhanced penalties.

Upon a finding by the factfinder that the defendant committed the charged offense for the purpose of benefiting, promoting, or furthering the interests of a criminal gang, the penalty for any felony or misdemeanor, or any delinquent act or violation of law which would be a felony or misdemeanor if committed by an adult, may be enhanced. Penalty enhancement affects the applicable statutory maximum penalty only. Each of the findings required as a basis for such sentence shall be found beyond a reasonable doubt. The enhancement will be as follows:

(1)(a) A misdemeanor of the second degree may be punished as if it were a misdemeanor of the first degree.

(b) A misdemeanor of the first degree may be punished as if it were a felony of the third degree. For purposes of sentencing under chapter 921 and determining incentive gain-time eligibility under chapter 944, such offense is ranked in level 1 of the offense severity ranking chart. The criminal gang multiplier in s. 921.0024 does not apply to misdemeanors enhanced under this paragraph.

(2)(a) A felony of the third degree may be punished as if it were a felony of the second degree.

(b) A felony of the second degree may be punished as if it were a felony of the first degree.

(c) A felony of the first degree may be punished as if it were a life felony.

Which of the following is true about enhanced penalties for gang-related offenses?

a. A third-degree felony is treated as a misdemeanor
b. A second-degree felony is treated as a third-degree felony
c. A first-degree misdemeanor is treated as a third-degree felony
d. A life felony is treated as a capital offense

9. Handicapped parking spaces:

In the case of a vehicle illegally parked in an official marked handicapped parking space, the responding officer must have the vehicle removed, either by the driver, or by an authorized tow truck. The vehicle can be removed to a municipal lot, a city garage, or a non-handicapped parking space. If the car's driver is nearby, the officer may order the person to move the vehicle. The officer shall cite the driver for parking in a handicapped parking space without the required permit.

At his/her discretion, the officer may order the driver to produce an official handicapped parking permit. If the officer does so, and the driver refuses to produce the permit, the officer may charge the driver with resisting an officer without violence.

Leaving a mall after investigating a shoplifting incident, you notice a car that doesn't have a handicapped parking permit parked in a handicapped parking space. As you leave your patrol car and approach the vehicle, a man comes out of the mall and approaches the car with keys in hand. You ask him for his disabled parking permit. He says he doesn't have one but since he's now leaving, it's no big deal.

Which of the following would NOT be a proper response by you?

a. Have the car towed and cite the man for illegal use of a handicapped space
b. Give the man a warning about parking in handicapped parking spaces without a permit
c. Cite the man for illegal use of a handicapped space
d. Order the man to move the car, cite him for illegal use of a handicapped space and arrest him for resisting an officer without violence

10. Police Vehicles Involved in Auto Accidents
1. The officer driving a police vehicle involved in any vehicular accident will:
  a. Allow all vehicles involved in the accident to remain in the post-accident position if traffic conditions permit. Except in emergencies, vehicles should not be moved from the scene.
  b. Render first aid (if needed) and arrange transportation for the injured (if needed).
  c. Immediately request Emergency Communication Center to send a district car and district/section/unit supervisor to investigate the accident.

You are patrolling a residential neighborhood. You've just pulled into a four-way intersection, after stopping at a stop sign, when a car comes from your right and collides with the rear passenger side of your patrol car, doing substantial damage. You are shaken up, but don't seem to have any injuries. The other driver is semi-conscious, and appears to be in serious pain, but there are no visible injuries. What should you do first?

a. Call for an ambulance
b. Render first aid
c. Call the ECC and request a district car and supervisor
d. Move the vehicles out of the roadway

Questions 11-13 are based on the following information:

Criminal trespass is defined as entering someone else's property without permission, or remaining on the property after being told to leave.

Burglary is defined as entering a building without the permission of the owner or tenant, for the purpose of committing a crime.

Theft is defined as taking someone else's property without their permission.

Home invasion is defined as forcefully entering an occupied dwelling for the purpose of committing a felony against one or more occupants.

11. A couple invites several friends and co-workers to their house for a football watching party. Unbeknownst to the couple, one of the invited co-workers is an ex-con. He has heard through the grapevine that the couple keeps a lot of valuables in the house, and he accepts their invitation in hopes of stealing something. Sometime during the party, he is caught in the act of pocketing a necklace from the jewelry box in the couple's bedroom. The couple calls the police. What should he be charged with?

a. Criminal trespass
b. Burglary
c. Theft
d. Home invasion

12. A man is out jogging in a residential neighborhood when he experiences severe stomach cramps. Seeing a home that appears to be unoccupied, he tries the front door, and it turns out to be unlocked. He goes in and uses the bathroom. While he's in the bathroom, the person who is renting the house comes home and discovers him there, and calls the police. What should he be charged with?

a. Criminal trespass
b. Burglary
c. Theft
d. Home invasion

13. Two men, Steve and Wayne, have been making plans to start a remodeling business as partners. However, the two have a serious falling out, and drop their plans to go into business together when Wayne accuses Steve of trying to take advantage of him financially. A few nights later Wayne and a couple of his friends show up at Steve's front door. They demand that Steve pay Wayne back for his "wasted time." Steve says he doesn't owe Wayne anything, and refuses to let them in. He orders them to leave. Instead, they kick the door in, and threaten to come back and beat Steve if he doesn't pay up within a week. Before they leave, they take some power tools from the garage and inform Steve he'll get them back when he pays what he owes. After they leave, Steve calls the police. What should Wayne and his friends be charged with?

a. Burglary
b. Home invasion
c. Criminal trespass and theft
d. Home invasion and theft

Questions 14 and 15 are based on the following information:

When dealing with a strike, picket line, or other dispute involving demonstrations or picketing, there is always a potential for things to quickly get out of control if police don't do their job properly. In such situations, a supervisor will meet with leaders or officials from both labor and management. The supervisor will inform both sides that the role of the police is to protect life and property, and that police officers cannot take either side in the dispute, but are there only to maintain public order and keep the peace.

The supervisor shall also explain to each side their rights, as well as the rights of the opposing side. They will also inform each side of its responsibilities in the situation, including the obligation to obey all laws, and to obey all lawful orders from police officers. Neither the supervisor nor any officer will under any circumstances discuss the dispute itself, or any other controversial matters, or state any opinion about labor, management, or the dispute.

If arrests are necessary, the following guidelines should be followed:

6. When it comes to shouting, "trash talking", etc., arrests should be kept to a minimum. Strive to prevent these behaviors from escalating, but arrests should be a last resort.
7. For minor disputes such as those above, the best tactic is to separate the offending parties, and order them to leave the area, with a warning that they will face arrest if they return.
8. When possible, arrests should be made immediately for assaults (threats), shoving, punching, or other instances of battery, intentionally damaging property, or inciting to riot.
9. In some situations an immediate arrest could lead to a situation getting out of hand—if it looks as if supporters are going to form a mob if you arrest a person, and there aren't enough officers on hand to deal with the situation, the situation could rapidly become dangerous to the public, yourself, and other officers. In a situation like this, it's best not to make an immediate arrest. Instead, note the perpetrator and make the arrest later when things are more under control.
10. Always stay on top of the situation and if it looks as if you may need more officers, call for them before they're needed. Simply having more officers arrive can often be enough to prevent things from escalating, or quickly bring violence to a halt.
11. If an arrest is necessary, remove the arrested person from the scene in order to prevent sympathizers from using him/her to stir up the crowd to engage in violence.

14. On a hot summer afternoon, you and another officer have been dispatched to a factory where around 100 angry workers have walked off the job and have formed a large and loud gathering near the entrance to the factory. Several managers stand between the crowd and the building and order the workers to come back in at once or risk being fired. Several of the workers approach you and your fellow officer demanding that the managers be arrested for violating their rights by not providing air conditioning. One of them is using extremely offensive language to describe the managers. They ask you if you think it's humane to make employees work in a factory without air conditioning. You should:

a. Arrest the person who is using foul language for disorderly conduct.
b. Agree that it's inhumane, but say that because it's not illegal, there's nothing you can do.
c. Take the managers aside and ask them to provide air conditioning for the workers.
d. Order the person using the foul language to leave the area or face arrest for disorderly conduct

15. In the same situation as Question 14, as you and your partner get out of your patrol car a manager waves you over. You both go over and speak to him. He says that one of the workers has damaged the building by spray painting some graffiti on it, which is clearly visible. He demands that you arrest the worker in question, who still has the paint can in his hand. The worker admits painting the graffiti and dares you to arrest him, and the crowd joins in, saying that if you try to arrest him you'll have to arrest all of them. You should:

a. Inform the manager that you can't take sides in the dispute so there's nothing you can do.
b. Make no arrests and call for backup.
c. Make no arrests and call for backup, and when enough officers are on the scene arrest the worker for the property damage.
d. Arrest the worker, after telling the crowd that anyone who tries to interfere will also be arrested.

Inductive Reasoning

1. One city passed a controversial ordinance in 2002, making it the law that if a person who had been named as the victim of a domestic assault refused to testify, they were required to undergo a minimum of three counseling sessions within six months or pay a $1000 fine. The city council said their immediate goal in passing the law was to encourage abuse victims not to give in to intimidation from their abusers, and their long-term goal was to reduce the incidence of domestic violence by sending more abusers to prison for a year or more. In 2010, the law was ruled unconstitutional by the courts, but we can look at several years of data to see if the law achieved its intended goals. Here are two charts that show the percentage of domestic abuse cases in which the victim refused to testify, and the number of cases of domestic abuse in which the abuser was sentenced to prison for a year or more, for several years after the law was passed.

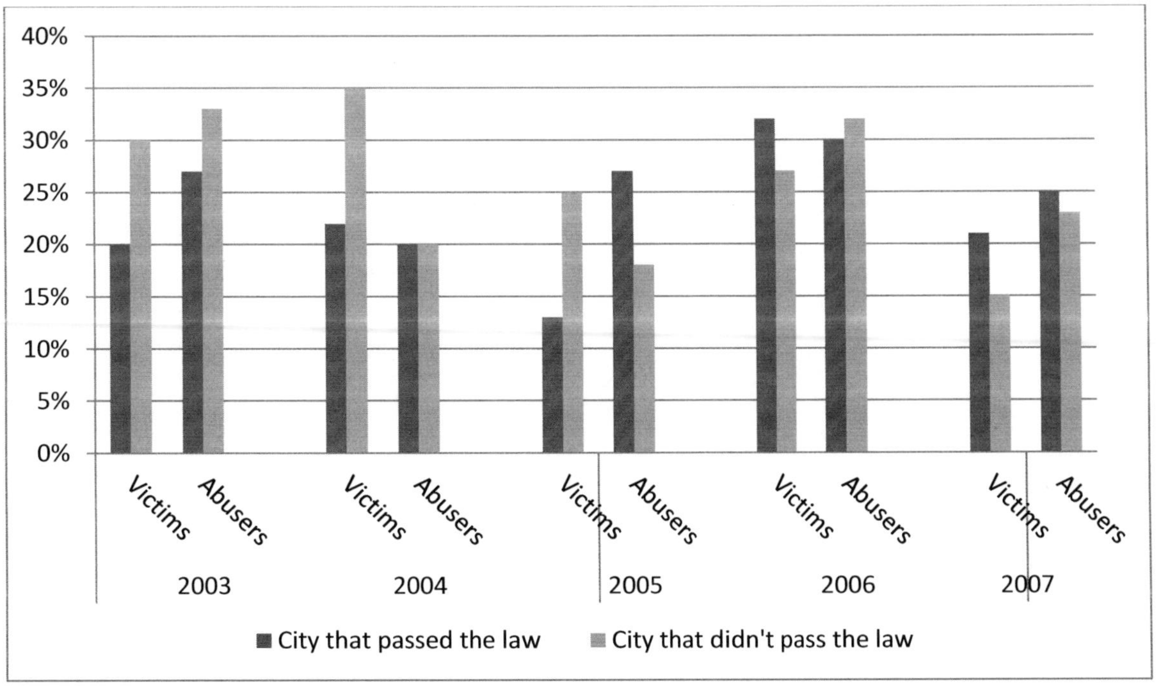

For the city that didn't pass the law, in which two years did the highest percentage of victims agree to testify?

a. 2005 and 2007
b. 2003 and 2005
c. 2005 and 2006
d. 2003 and 2007

2. After a string of several high-profile car wrecks caused by drunk drivers resulted in the deaths of multiple children during the holiday season one year, the city council decided to focus their efforts on reducing the number of bartenders who are willing to serve customers who've had too much to drink. They passed a law requiring all establishments that serve alcohol to prominently display a poster urging customers to call a hotline and turn in bartenders who continue to serve customers who are clearly drunk. During the first year, exactly one hundred people called the hotline to report a bartender serving a drunken customer. Here is a chart breaking down the calls by month.

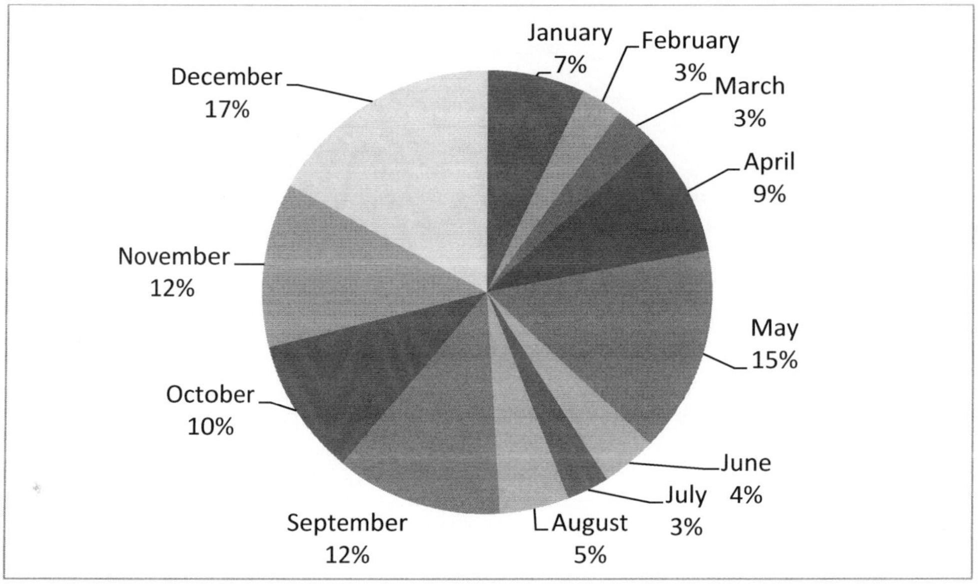

In which month did the greatest number of people call the hotline?

a. November
b. September
c. May
d. December

3. Here is a chart of major crimes in one American city for the years 2001, 2005, 2009, and 2013.

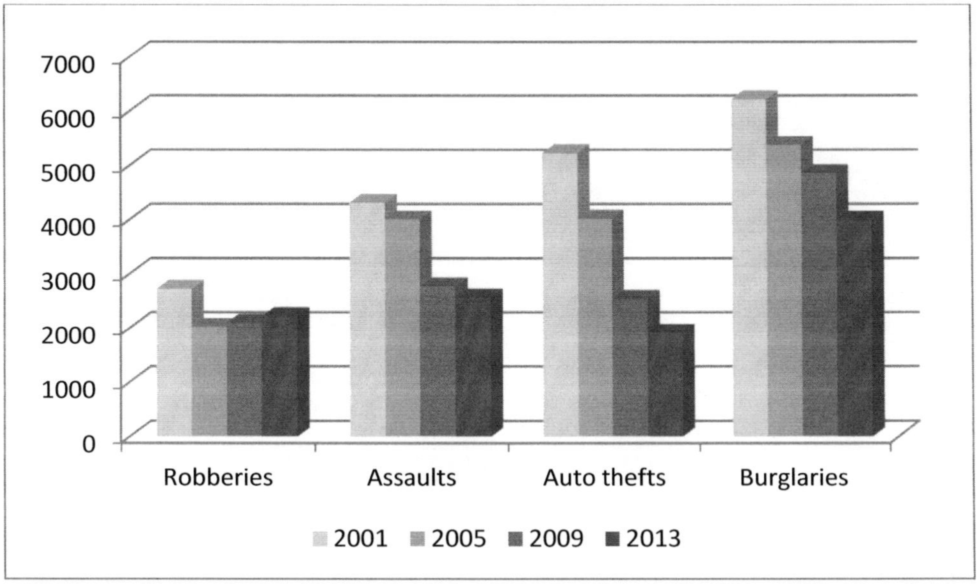

In which year were there fewer auto thefts than robberies?

a. 2001
b. 2005
c. 2009
d. 2013

4. Here is some data about sex abusers in one city, showing the categories of relationships sexual abusers have with their victims, and what percentage of abusers are in each category, for the years 2011 and 2014.

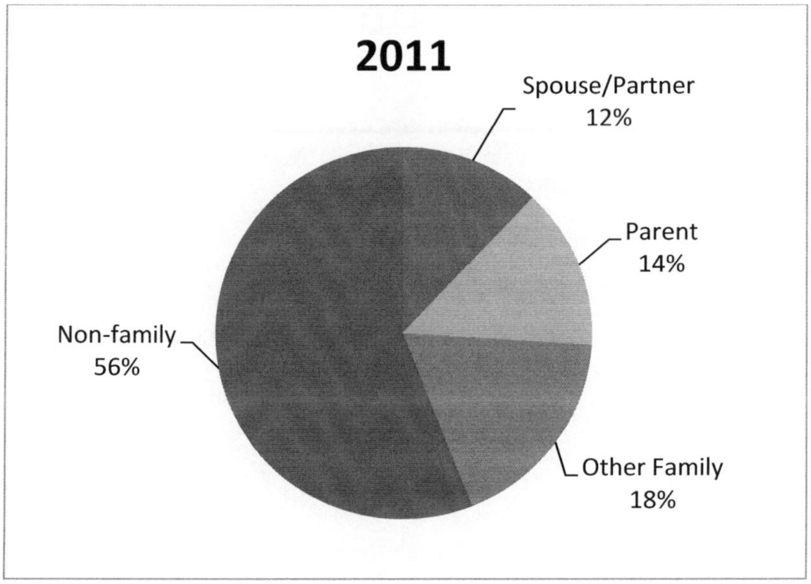

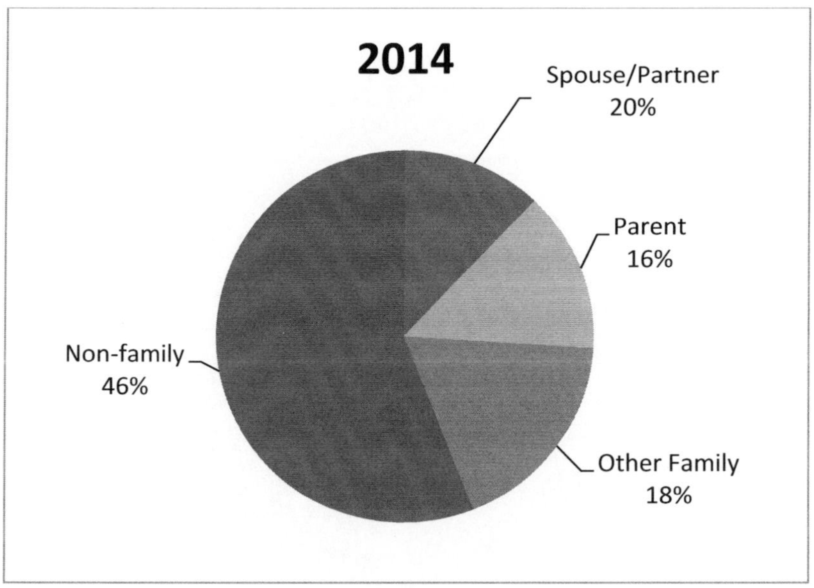

In 2014, which category saw the biggest increase from 2011?

a. Spouse/Partner
b. Parent
c. Other family
d. Non-family

5. Here are two pie charts showing the geographic origins of all undocumented immigrants arrested for being in the country illegally for the years 2010 and 2011 in one major city.

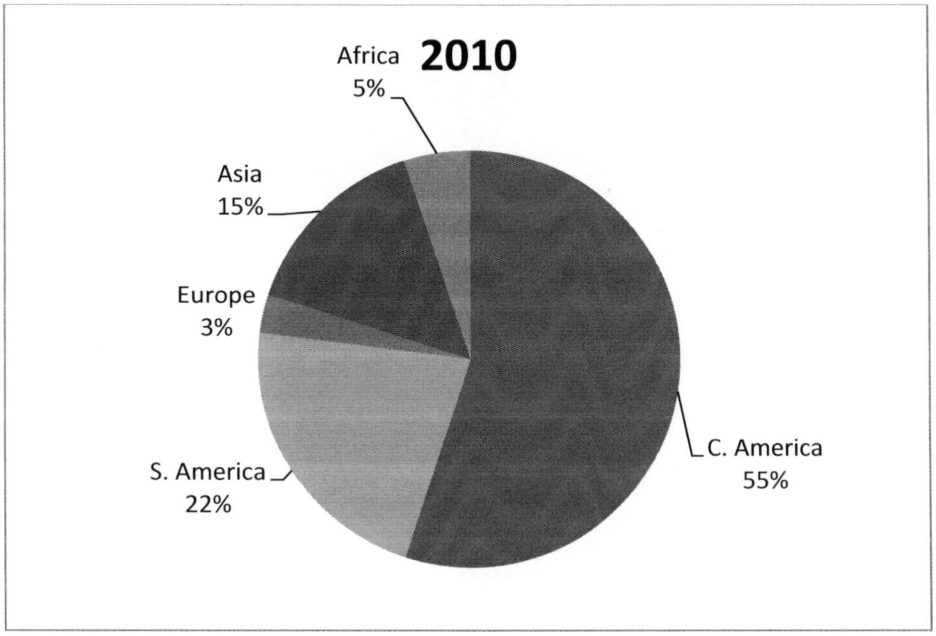

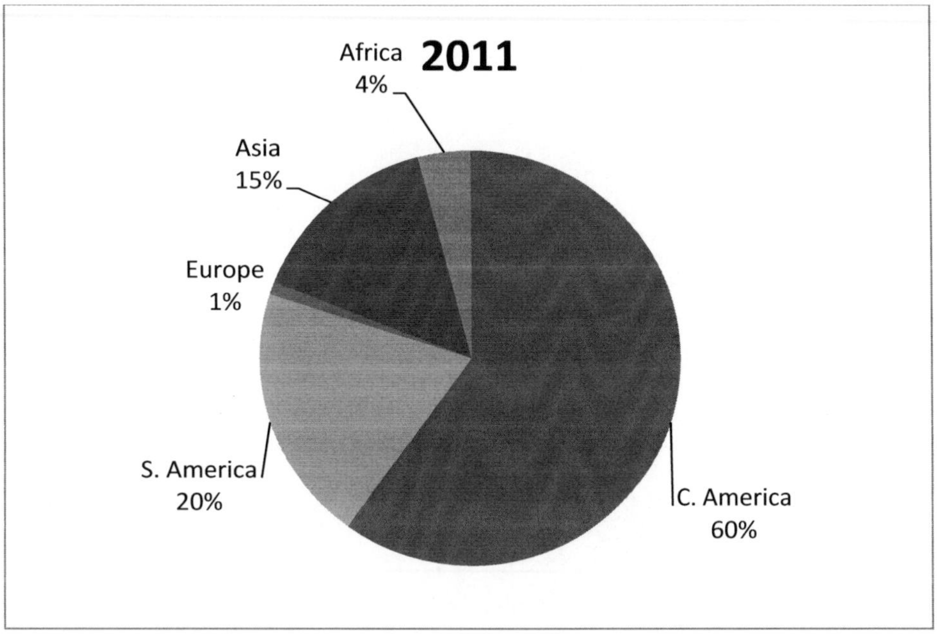

Which geographic area accounted for the same percentage of undocumented workers in both years?

a. Asia
b. Europe
c. South America
d. Central America

6. There is no longer any argument about whether or not red-light cameras reduce red-light running. The evidence is in, and they clearly do. However, experts say that they should not be installed at an intersection merely because a lot of people run red lights there. Two factors should exist at the intersection before installing a red-light camera—drivers running red lights at a rate at least 25% higher than at the average light, and a percentage of accidents caused by people running red lights that is at least 10% higher than at the average traffic light. There are six intersections being considered for red light cameras.

Intersection	Red-Light Runners	Red-Light Running Accidents
1	1.10	0.95
2	1.25	1.00
3	0.95	1.25
4	1.25	1.15
5	1.10	1.10
6	1.30	1.10

In the table above, Column 2 shows the percentage of drivers who run the red light as a percentage of the average number of drivers who run red lights at all intersections. Column 3 shows the percentage of accidents at that intersection which were caused by people running red lights, compared to the average number of accidents caused by people running red lights at all intersections. Percentages are expressed in decimal form, so 1.0 is average, 1.50 is 50% above average, 0.75 is 25% below average, etc. Using the above standards, which two intersections above should get red light cameras?

a. 2 and 5
b. 4 and 6
c. 1 and 4
d. 5 and 6

7. The city manager is considering outfitting all patrol cars with new emergency light systems. One company says their design incorporates a newly developed system of colors and patterns that can significantly improve visibility, reducing delays and accidents involving patrol cars. The city manager agreed to install the system on four patrol cars for 30 days, and if at the end of the trial response times for those four cars have been cut by an average of 15 seconds or more, she will authorize the purchase of a system for all patrol cars.

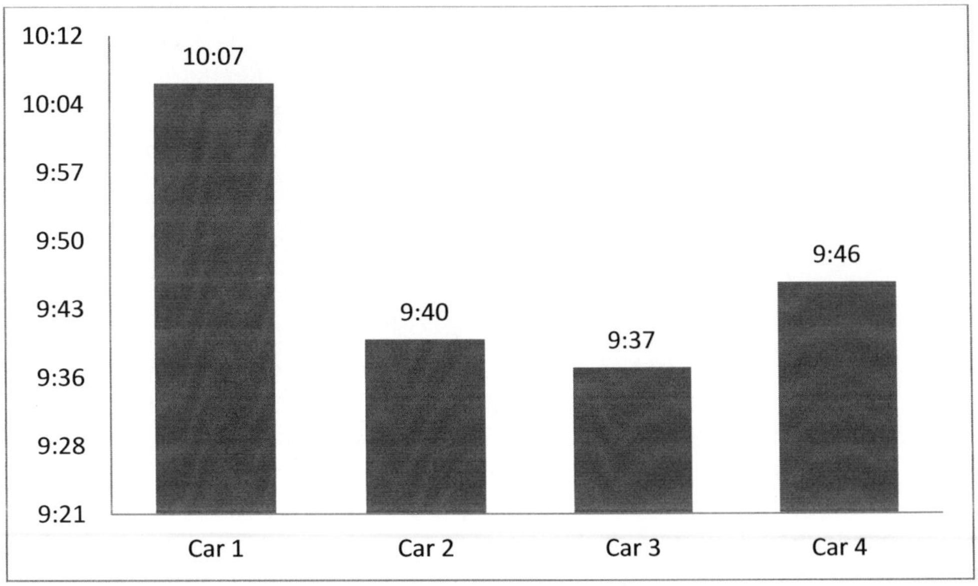

The benchmark, or the average response time before the trial that the test results would be measured against, was 10:00. At the end of the trial, Car 1 had an average response time of 10:07, Car 2 had an average response time of 9:40, Car 3 had an average response time of 9:37, and Car 4 had an average response time of 9:46. Which of the following is true of the average response time of the cars in the trial?

a. It was lower than the benchmark by 15.5 seconds
b. It was higher than the benchmark by 15.5 seconds
c. It was lower than the benchmark by 12.5 seconds
d. It was higher than the benchmark by 12.5 seconds

8. After learning that its budget wouldn't increase from the previous year due to municipal belt-tightening, the police department in one city was looking for ways to be more effective without spending more money. They decided to park empty patrol cars near stretches of roads which had high accident rates due to speeding. The empty cars would be close enough to be a visible deterrent, but far enough away from the road that it wasn't obvious that the cars were empty. At first, this worked well, and the accident rate declined for a few months. However, drivers eventually realized that the cars were empty, and speed picked up again, as did the accident rate. Then the department began randomly posting officers in cars where the empty cars had been and rotating between manned and unmanned cars on an unpredictable basis. It took a few months, but after drivers began to realize that they could never be sure if the patrol cars were manned or not, they began slowing down again, and the accident rate once again declined.

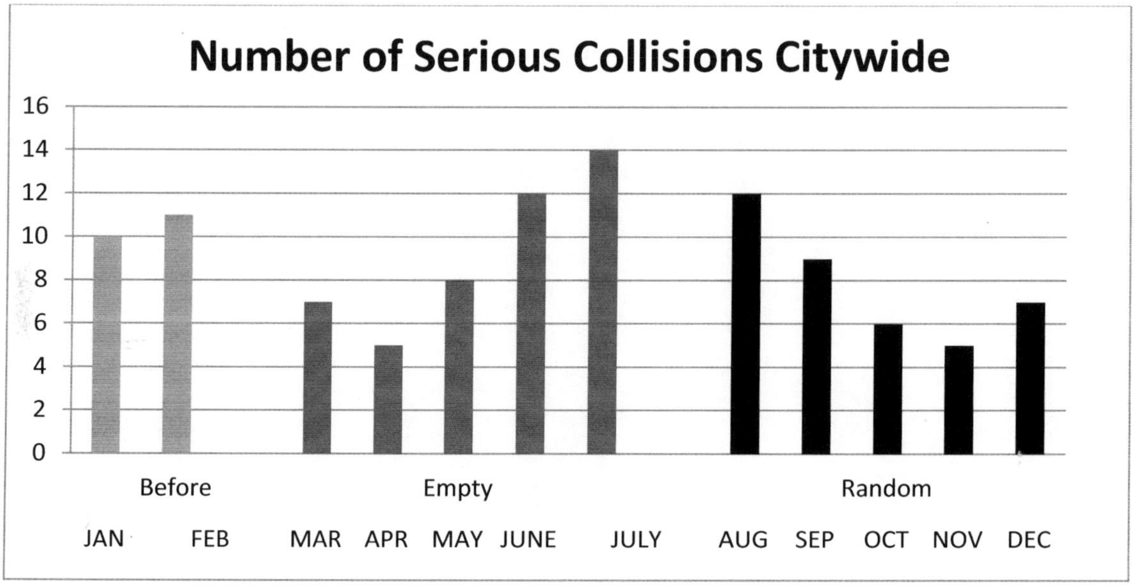

Which of these pairs of months had the same number of accidents?

a. January and September
b. February and June
c. May and November
d. June and August

9. Preventing people from smuggling contraband to prisoners is one of the most difficult but most important functions a prison administration is charged with, but it's a never-ending battle. In one state, an experiment was tried in hopes of reducing contraband smuggling—at half the prisons, a change was made to the sign which is posted at the visitor's entrance to every facility. The sign, which is 12 inches tall and 6 inches wide, and designed with bold colors, says: BRINGING CONTRABAND INTO THIS FACILITY IS A FELONY PUNISHABLE BY UP TO TWO YEARS IN PRISON. IF YOU HAVE CONTRABAND ON YOUR PERSON, DO NOT ENTER THIS FACILITY. IF YOU DO ENTER, YOU WILL BE SEARCHED, AND IF FOUND IN POSSESSION OF CONTRABAND, YOU WILL BE PUNISHED TO THE FULLEST EXTENT OF THE LAW.

At half of the state prisons, the size of the sign was increased to 36 inches tall and 18 inches wide. At the other prisons, no change to the sign was made. Otherwise, policies at all prisons were exactly the same—all visitors were searched, and all visitors possessing contraband were arrested and prosecuted. Here are the charts showing the number of contraband items discovered on visitors for the four quarters following the posting of the larger signs. Group A facilities had the new signage; Group B facilities had the old signage.

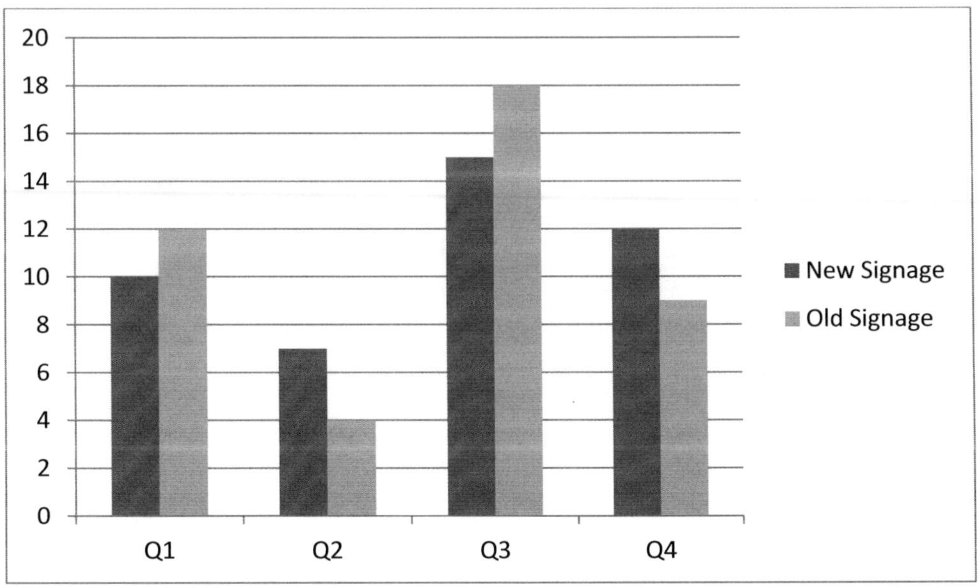

In which quarter was the difference between the two sets of facilities the greatest on a percentage basis?

a. Q1
b. Q2
c. Q3
d. Q4

10. There have been a string of armed robberies near a park over the past few weeks. Police believe most of them are the work of the same person. Here are suspect descriptions from the victim in each mugging.

Robbery	Height	Race	Age	Unique Identifiers
Robbery 1	6'0"	White	App. 30	Victim doesn't
Robbery 2	5'10"	White	Late 20s	Tattoo on left arm; possibly eagle
Robbery 3	6'2"	White	25-30	Possible tattoo on one arm
Robbery 4	5'7"	White	25-30	Large knife scar down left cheek

Which one of the robberies most likely wasn't committed by the same person?

a. 1
b. 2
c. 3
d. 4

11. This chart from the United States Department of Health and Human Services shows the percentage of people in each age bracket who have driven under the influence of alcohol at least once during the past 12 months.

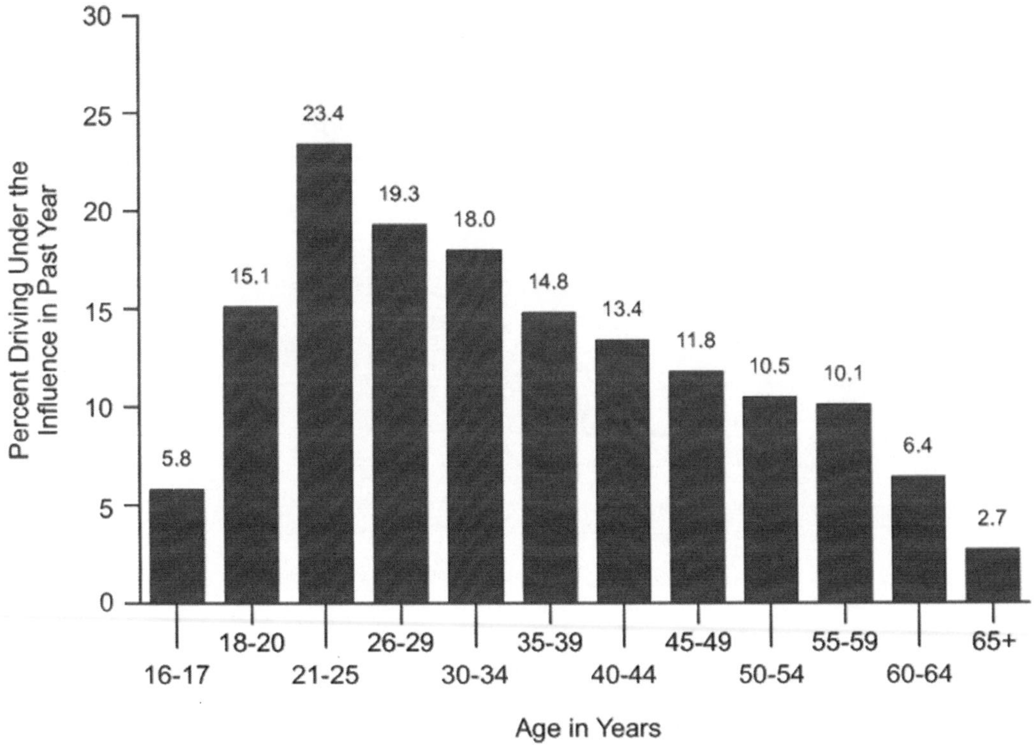

Which age bracket is third highest when it comes to the most people who have driven under the influence of alcohol in the past 12 months?

a. 18-20
b. 26-29
c. 30-34
d. 35-39

12. This chart from the United States Department of Health and Human Services shows the percentage of young people who reported that they had used alcohol in the past 30 days, broken down by age bracket and year.

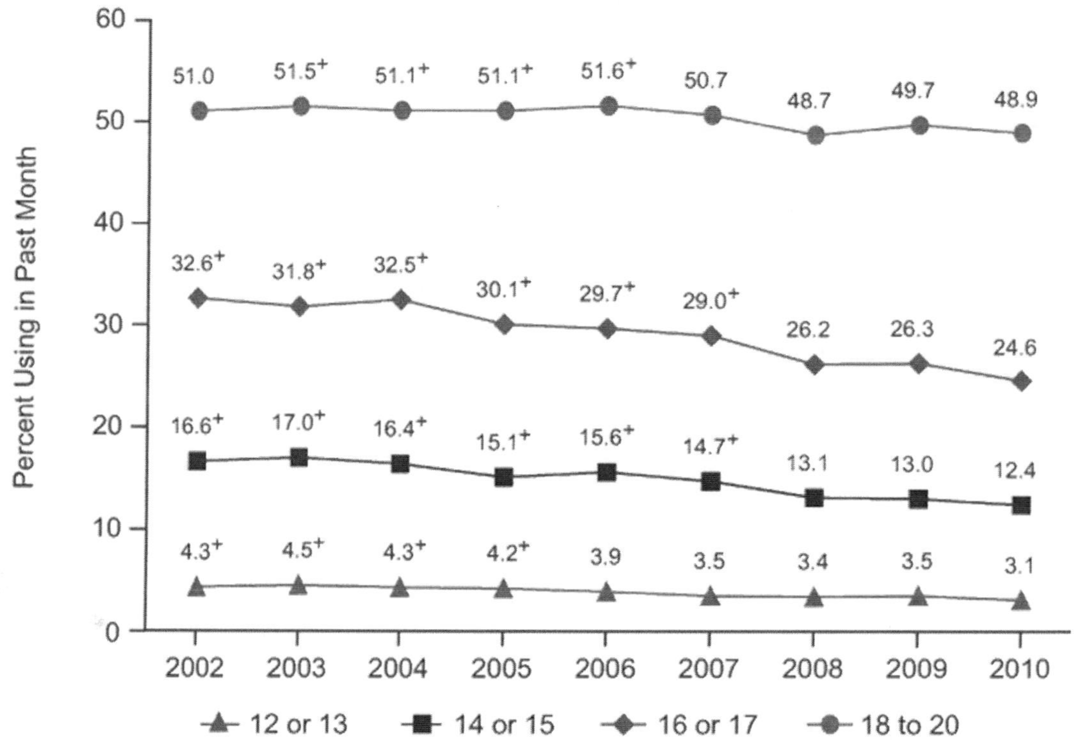

Which year had the highest percentage of 12–13-year-olds reporting alcohol use in the past 30 days?

a. 2009
b. 2006
c. 2003
d. 2005

13. Until recently, many local law enforcement agencies in one state required a minimum of an associate's degree for police academy recruits. After the state legislature passed a law setting new standards, all agencies in the state now require applicants to have a bachelor's degree (or higher). The number of recruits has plummeted. Here are the figures for four cities in the state. The first bar shows the number of applicants for the city's academy in 2012; the second bar is the number who applied in 2013.

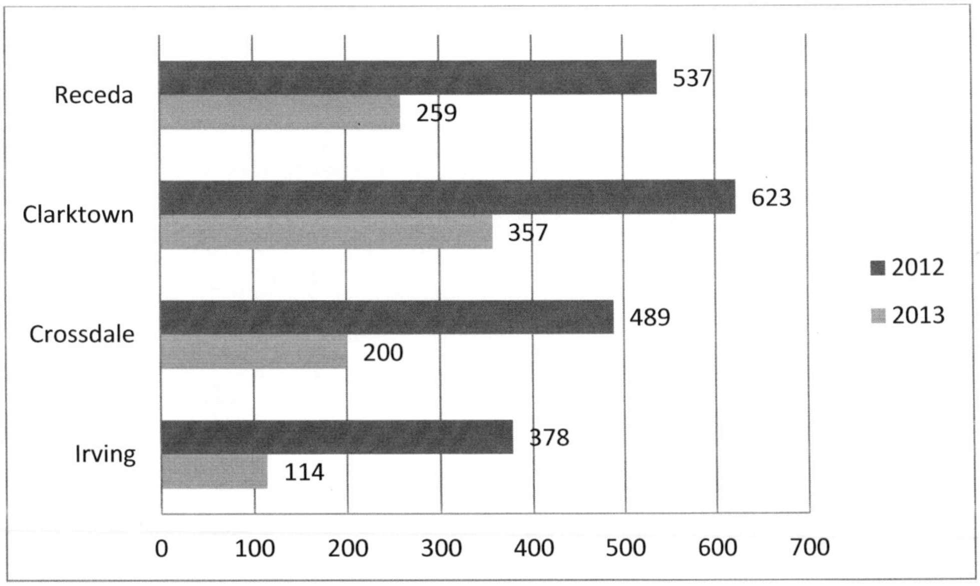

Which city experienced the greatest percentage decline in applicants in 2013?

a. Irving
b. Crossdale
c. Clarktown
d. Receda

14. This table shows the racial/ethnic breakdown of corrections officers at four facilities:

Facility	African American	Asian American	Hispanic	White
Milton	18%	2%	14%	66%
Ferguson	15%	2%	28%	55%
Dalton	32%	4%	30%	34%
Howard	12%	12%	24%	52%

Assuming each facility employs 200 officers, at which facility is the combined number of Asian-American and Hispanic officers equal to the number of white officers?

a. Milton
b. Ferguson
c. Dalton
d. Howard

15. Four correctional facilities recently held their annual physical exam for officers. Here is a table showing how many officers at each facility were told they need to lose weight, broken down by age range. Assuming each facility employs 50 officers in each age range, which facility has the most corrections officers that need to lose weight?

Facility	22-30	31-40	41-50	50+
Milton	6%	10%	4%	22%
Ferguson	20%	18%	22%	22%
Dalton	14%	10%	24%	30%
Howard	4%	6%	20%	36%

a. Milton
b. Ferguson
c. Dalton
d. Howard

Information Ordering

1. You are off duty and have just been seated with your family in a restaurant where, at a nearby table, a young mother is dining with her nine-month-old infant. Suddenly the mother yells that the infant is choking on her food. Put the following steps of your response in order.

   1. If back thumps and chest compressions have both failed, call 911.
   2. While waiting for emergency responders, begin infant CPR.
   3. Take a seat in a nearby chair, and place the baby face down on your forearm, which is supported by your thigh.
   4. If the back thumps don't work, then, using your forearm, hold the baby face up, head lower than trunk, and placing your fingers at the center of the breastbone, give five short chest compressions.
   5. Using the heel of your hand, thump the baby firmly (but gently) in the middle of its back, five times in a row. This should dislodge the food.

   a. 1,5,3,4,2
   b. 2,1,3,4,5
   c. 5,1,2,4,3
   d. 3,5,4,1,2

2. Put the following events from a crime victim's statement in chronological order.

   1. A man came out of an alley with a gun and demanded my wallet.
   2. He struck me in the head with the butt of his gun and then took off running.
   3. I didn't have my phone with me, so I asked a passerby to call the police and report the crime.
   4. I gave him my wallet.
   5. I was walking down the street minding my own business.

   a. 5,1,4,2,3
   b. 1,3,4,5,2
   c. 5,2,4,1,3
   d. 5,3,2,4,1

3. You have been called to a store about a shoplifting incident. Put these statements from the assistant manager of the store in chronological order.

   1. With his cart full, he left the store without paying.
   2. He left the clothing department and proceeded to the toy department and loaded several expensive toys into his cart.
   3. Security alerted me that a person with a history of shoplifting had entered the store.
   4. I went to our CCTV room and watched him as he put several items of men's clothing in his cart.
   5. Two security guards apprehended him in the parking lot and detained him, and I called for your assistance.

   a. 3,2,1,4,5
   b. 3,4,2,1,5
   c. 4,3,1,2,5
   d. 3,1,2,4,5

4. On occasion, law enforcement officers will respond to a call and discover that a crime in progress has turned into a hostage situation. When this occurs, the officers should take the following steps (in order, when possible):

1. Order all passersby away from the building.
2. Assign officers (if available) to divert pedestrian and vehicular traffic from the immediate vicinity.
3. If you have enough available officers to cover all ground floor exits, assign at least one officer to each one
4. Ask dispatch to send a hostage negotiator (and additional officers if necessary).
5. Attempt to establish communication with the hostage taker, either directly or by phone, while waiting for the hostage negotiator to arrive.

You and your partner have arrived at a house to respond to a domestic dispute, but as you approach the house a man yells that he has a gun and will kill his wife if you come any further. You and your partner retreat from the house. There are no pedestrians or onlookers. Your partner posts at the entrance to the cul-de-sac to block incoming traffic. What is your next step?

a. Attempt to establish communication with the hostage taker, either directly or by phone, while waiting for the hostage negotiator to arrive.
b. Assign at least one officer (if available) to the outside of each door or window on the ground floor.
c. Assign officers (if available) to divert pedestrian and vehicular traffic from the immediate vicinity.
d. Ask dispatch to send a hostage negotiator and additional officers.

5. According to FBI hostage negotiation experts' Behavioral Change Stairway Model, there are five stages that must occur when negotiating with a hostage. They are:

1. Active Listening – you listen to the criminal and let them know you hear and understand them, and you don't interrupt while they're talking
2. Empathy – you try to mentally put yourself in their position to understand where they're coming from
3. Rapport – when you listen and show empathy, the criminal begins to trust you. You have established rapport.
4. Influence – Once rapport is established, you attempt to reason with them and work out a solution to the situation.
5. Behavioral Change – this is when the criminal takes action in response to the previous steps; the desired action is releasing the hostage and surrendering peacefully.

As in the previous question, you and your partner have arrived at a house to respond to a domestic dispute, but as you approach the house a man yells that he has a gun and will kill his wife if you come any closer. Your law enforcement agency is small, and doesn't have a trained hostage negotiator, and it falls on you to begin talking to the man in an attempt to convince him to let his wife go and surrender peacefully. As you talk to him, and he begins telling you how hopeless things are for him in life, you respond by telling him that you know it looks hopeless, but things can change, because you've been through bad situations yourself.

Which stage are you in when you're talking about a time when things looked bad for you?

a. Active Listening
b. Empathy
c. Influence
d. Behavioral Change

6. Below are the five steps a law enforcement agency has established for dealing with a person who has not committed a crime, but is suspected of being mentally ill and who is likely to injure himself/herself and/or others.

1. Identify yourself and your law enforcement agency
2. Take the person into custody
3. Explain that the person is not being arrested or charged with a crime
4. Inform the person that they are being taken to a facility to be examined by mental health professionals
5. Transport the person to the appropriate mental health facility and check him or her in

You have responded to a complaint about a man acting in a bizarre manner in a quiet neighborhood. When you get there, you see a disheveled looking man shouting nonsensically and gesturing wildly. You approach the man, who doesn't appear to have a weapon. What should you do next?

a. Tell him that he's not under arrest.
b. Identify yourself and your law enforcement agency.
c. Place him in handcuffs as quickly as possible.
d. Wait for backup.

7. During a Firearms Inspection, the Firearms Inspector will:

1. Retrieve an officer's firearm, make sure that it is empty, and insert a specially modified magazine provided by the Firearms Training Unit into the well of the firearm.
2. Allow the slide to go forward and aim the weapon into the clearing trap, and pull the trigger in order to make sure the trigger is functioning properly. If it is not, the firearm should be taken to the department firing range to be examined by an armorer.
3. If the trigger is working correctly, pull the slide back in order to again engage the trigger and put the bullet blocker in the barrel. If the bullet blocker shows green, the weapon is unloaded. If it shows red, it means there is an obstruction in the gun's barrel, and the inspector should attempt to locate and remove it. If the inspector is unable to remove the obstruction, the firearm should be taken to the department firing range to be examined by an armorer.
4. If the bullet blocker shows green, aim the weapon at the ceiling and pull the trigger. If the firearm is in good working condition, this will send the bullet blocker a short distance upward. If it doesn't, the firearm should be taken to the department firing range to be examined by an armorer.
5. If the bullet blocker is ejected, give the firearm back to the officer.

If the trigger isn't functioning properly, which of these would be the last step taken before sending the firearm to be examined by an armorer?

a. 1
b. 2
c. 3
d. 4

8. Put these procedures for using the Mobile Command Center (MCC) in order:

1. Complete Form 362, documenting any damage the MCC sustained while in your custody.
2. Obtain official approval before using the MCC.
3. Fill out the sign-out log form in full before starting up the MCC and leaving the facility.
4. Notify Tactical Fleet Unit when the MCC is no longer needed and on its way back to the hangar.
5. Notify Tactical Fleet Unit when the MCC is powered up on location.

a. 5,1,3,2,4
b. 2,1,5,4,3
c. 2,3,5,4,1
d. 3,2,5,4,1

9. A police department has issued these basic procedures for a supervisor to follow at the scene of a homicide. Put them in order:

1. He or she will then examine the body, and interview the officer or officers who were first on the scene.
2. The supervisor will either remain on the crime scene until the Homicide Unit has finished processing the scene, or he or she will designate another supervisor to take command before leaving the scene.
3. After getting the basic information from the officers, the supervisor will make sure that no one else enters the scene until the Homicide Unit arrives.
4. The first supervisor to arrive on the scene will take command.
5. After the Homicide Unit arrives, the supervisor will then assign an officer to complete Form 95, logging all information about any personnel allowed to enter the crime scene, the time of their entrance, the reason they were approved for entry, and the time they left the scene. 2) The supervisor will either remain on the crime scene until the Homicide Unit has finished processing the scene, or he or she will designate another supervisor to take command before leaving the scene.

a. 3,2,4,1,5
b. 3,4,5,1,2
c. 4,1,3,5,2
d. 4,2,1,3,5

10. These are your department's official procedures for submitting pills and capsules as drug evidence for analysis. Put them in their proper order.

1. Seal the bag and weigh it.
2. Weigh the pills before bagging.
3. After weight and count are written on the bag, mark the bag with the names and badge numbers of both the officer and the supervisor.
4. On the outside of the bag, write the number of pills, the weight before bagging, and the weight including the bag.
5. Put the pills in an official evidence bag.

a. 2,5,1,4,3
b. 2,1,5,4,3
c. 5,2,1,4,3
d. 1,3,4,2,5

11. Put these procedures for Road Squad Preparations in order:

The Lead Correctional Officer will:

1. Make sure the Road Squad van is inspected for contraband and that it is both safe and mechanically reliable before any inmates are loaded.
2. Notify the Officer-in-Charge of the location of the day's work site and request a Road Squad van.
3. Assign an officer to drive the inspected Road Squad van to the inmate pickup area.
4. Conduct a head count and roll call before leaving the work site to return to the facility.
5. Make sure that each inmate assigned to the Road Squad is completely searched before leaving the facility to enter the Road Squad van.

a. 1,2,3,4,5
b. 2,1,3,4,5
c. 2,1,3,5,4
d. 3,1,2,5,4

12. These are some of your department's official procedures for dealing with junk or abandoned vehicles. Put them in the correct order.

1. When 48 hours have passed, attach an Abandoned Vehicle Sticker (AVS) to the driver's side window.
2. Run the vehicle's license plate and vehicle identification numbers through the system to locate the owner.
3. Mark the tires to start the 48-hour window the owner has to move the vehicle.
4. Attempt to contact the owner to tell them to move the vehicle. If unsuccessful, proceed to next step.
5. Enter the AVS serial number into the Abandoned Vehicle Log.

a. 5,3,2,1,4
b. 2,4,5,3,1
c. 2,4,3,1,5
d. 3,2,1,4,5

13. False alarms from home alarm systems are a growing problem for police departments across the country, and many cities are now fining homeowners if their system causes police to respond to a false alarm. Here is the outline of procedures for one department's False Alarms Response Unit (FARU). Put them in order.

FARU will:

1. Send a bill to the homeowner or business owner for the false alarm as authorized by City Ordinance 10-5927.
2. Amend the False Alarm Report record as necessary to match the ECC summary.
3. Double check every False Alarm Report for completeness and accuracy as soon as received.
4. Compare the False Alarm Report with the official computerized summary of alarm runs from the ECC.
5. Enter the information from the False Alarm Report into the alarm billing system database.

a. 1,3,2,4,5
b. 3,2,4,5,1
c. 2,4,3,5,1
d. 3,4,2,5,1

14. Here are the procedures established by the police department of a large city for dealing with snow emergencies:

1. After being notified by the City Manager that an official snow emergency has been declared, Emergency Communications Center (ECC) will record the time the notification was received, and will then inform the Patrol Bureau Commander, or their designated substitute, and all police units by radio and teletype, that an official snow emergency is in effect.
2. ECC will then inform the city's Director of Communications, who will become the official spokesperson and media liaison for the city for the duration of the snow emergency.
3. ECC will then inform newspapers, radio stations, and television stations, via email and voicemail, that a snow emergency has been declared. They will also post this information on various forms of social media.
4. ECC will notify the on-duty Traffic Unit supervisor of the snow emergency, who will become the snow emergency vehicle removal detail supervisor.
5. Finally, ECC will request two wreckers from the rotation list for each District be deployed to the Public Services Garage, at a time determined by the Public Services Department.

In which of these sequences is the step in which citizens would be able to read the official snow emergency declaration on Facebook in the correct spot in the sequence?

a. 1,2,4,5,3
b. 2,4,5,3,1
c. 5,1,3,2,4
d. 4,3,2,1,5

15. A Spontaneous Alert will be initiated when a riot or other civil unrest breaks out unexpectedly. In the event of a Spontaneous Alert, Emergency Command Center will:

1. In the Computer Dispatch System (CDS) display, highlight each Hostile Area as reports of hostilities come in.
2. Notify all non-essential personnel on the Spontaneous Alert notification list.
3. Dispatch cars to a Hostile Area only when requested by the Officer-in-Charge of that Hostile Area.
4. Notify all essential personnel in all sections, districts, and units, using both radio and teletype, that a Spontaneous Alert is in effect.
5. Order all officers on routine runs to cancel their runs and await further instructions.

Which of these shows the correct order of the above procedures?

a. 4,2,5,1,3
b. 5,4,2,1,3
c. 3,4,1,2,5
d. 1,4,2,3.5

Spatial Orientation

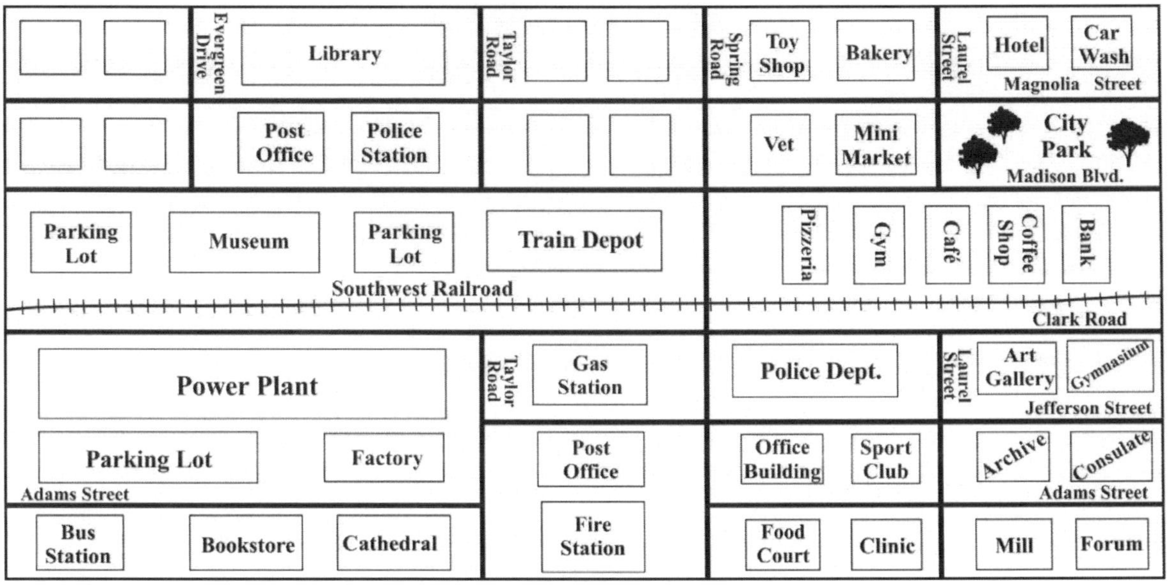

1. Officer Chavez is between the hotel and the car wash when he is dispatched to investigate a car accident in front of the parking lot of the power plant. Which of these would be the shortest route between the hotel and the power plant parking lot?

a. Drive south on Spring Road, west on Jefferson Street, south on Taylor Road, and west on Adams Street.
b. Drive west on Clark Road, south on Laurel Street, east on Jefferson Street, south on Spring Road, and east on Adams Street,
c. Drive west on Magnolia Street, south on Taylor Road, east on Madison Boulevard, south on Spring Road, west on Jefferson Street, south on Taylor Road, and west on Adams Street.
d. Drive west on Magnolia Street, south on Spring Road, west on Clark Road, south on Taylor Road, and west on Adams Street.

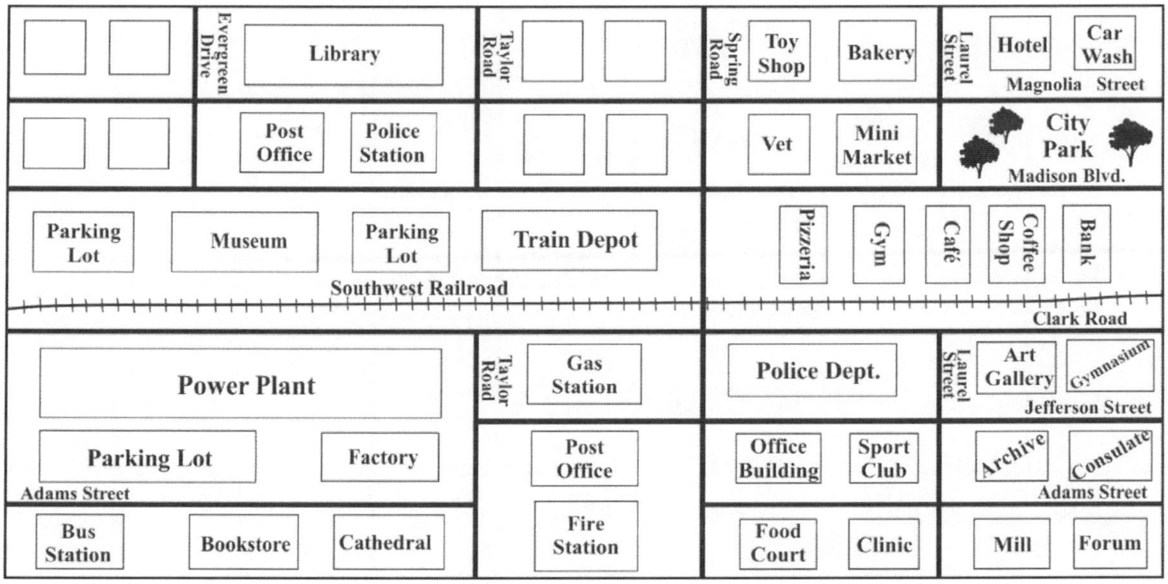

2. Officer Randall is at the Post Office that is one block south of the library, and needs to get to the art gallery to investigate a break-in. Which of these would be the shortest route between the Post Office and the art gallery?

a. Drive north on Taylor Road, east on Magnolia Street, south on Spring Road, and east on Jefferson Street.
b. Drive west on Jefferson Street, north on Spring Road, and west on Madison Boulevard.
c. Drive east on Madison Boulevard, south on Spring Road, and east on Jefferson Street.
d. Drive east on Madison Boulevard, south on Spring Road, and east on Adams Street.

3. If an officer is on patrol between the archive and the mill, and is dispatched to the bus station, which of these is the shortest route between these two points?

a. Drive north on Spring Road, drive west on Magnolia Street, and south on Clark Road.
b. Drive west on Adams Street, north on Spring Road, west on Jefferson Street, south on Taylor Road, and west on Adams Street.
c. Drive east on Adams Street, north on Taylor Road, east on Jefferson Street, south on Spring Road, and east on Adams Street.
d. Drive east on Jefferson Street, north on Laurel Street, west on Clark Road, and south on Spring Road.

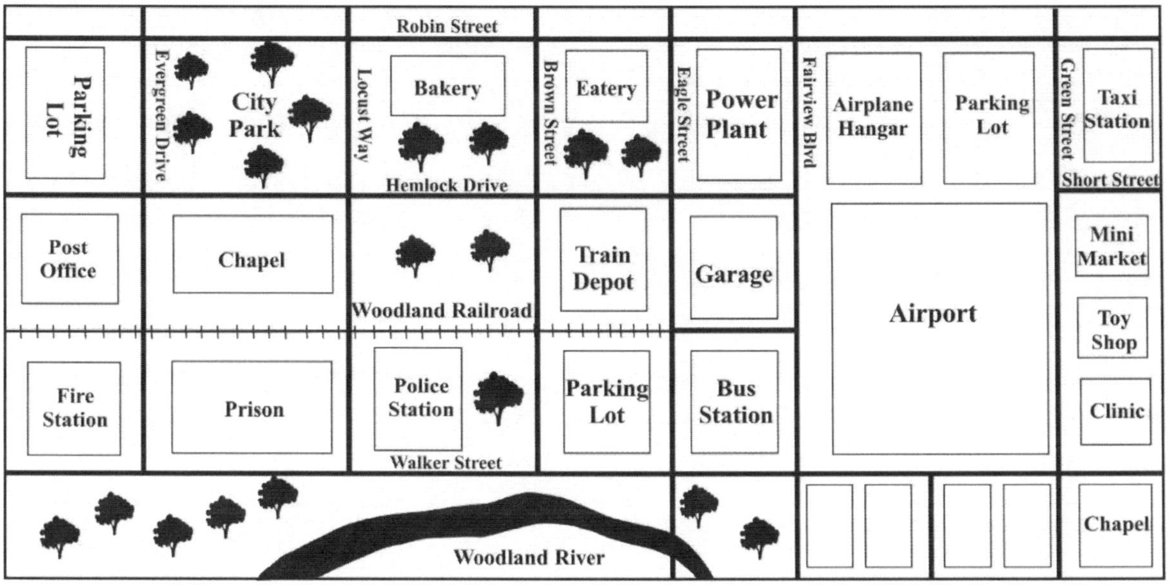

4. A suspected shoplifter has been detained at the toy store. The officers dispatched to arrest the suspect are just finishing up their lunch at the eatery next to the power plant. Which of these is the shortest route from there to the toy store?

a. Drive south on Eagle Street, east on Hemlock Drive, south on Fairview Boulevard, east on Walker Street, and north on Green Street.
b. Drive north on Brown Street, east on Robin Street, and south on Green Street.
c. Drive north on Green Street, west on Robin Street, and south on Brown Street.
d. Drive east on Hemlock Drive, north on Fairview Boulevard, east on Robin Street, and south on Green Street.

5. If an officer needs to get from the taxi station to the fire station, which of these is the shortest route?

a. Drive west on Robin Street and south on Evergreen Drive
b. Drive east on Robin Street and south on Evergreen Drive
c. Drive south on Fairview Boulevard and west on Hemlock Drive
d. Drive north on Evergreen Drive and west on Robin Street

6. Officers are patrolling the area between the bus station and the Woodland River when they are dispatched to investigate a disturbance at the city park. Which of these is the shortest route between these two points?

a. Drive south on Fairview Boulevard and east on Robin Street
b. Drive north on Fairview Boulevard and west on Robin Street
c. Drive north on Eagle Street and west on Hemlock Drive
d. Drive north on Walker Street and west on Evergreen Drive

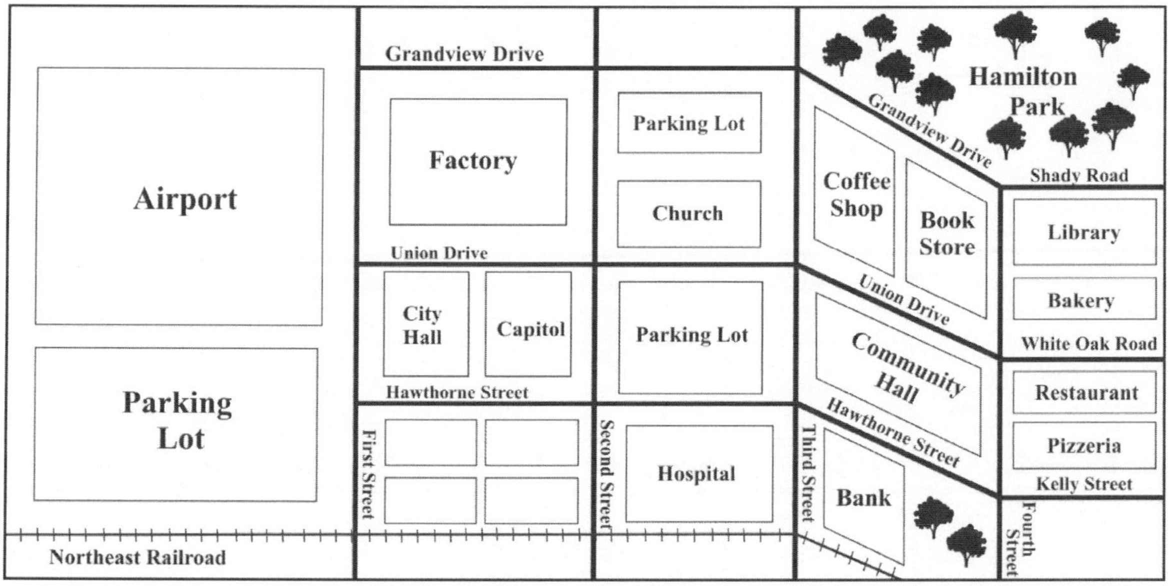

7. Officers Hazelwood and Rankin have been dispatched to the factory about a heated argument in a picket line on the north side of the plant. They are currently parked on the north side of the library. Which of these is the shortest route between where they're parked and the factory?

a. Drive north on Second Street and west on Union Drive.
b. Drive west on Shady Road and west on Grandview Drive.
c. Drive north on Fourth Street and west on Grandview Drive.
d. Drive west on Shady Road, south on Fourth Street and west on Union Drive.

8. Officer Johnson is patrolling Hamilton Park when his assistance is requested at the hospital. Which of these is the shortest route between his location and the hospital?

a. Drive east on Hawthorne Street, north on Fourth Street, and east on Shady Road
b. Drive west on Shady Road, south on Fourth Street, west on Union Drive, and south on Second Street.
c. Drive west on Shady Road, south on Fourth Street, and west on Hawthorne Street.
d. Drive west on Shady Road, northwest on Grandview Drive, south on Third Street, west on Union Drive, and south on Second Street.

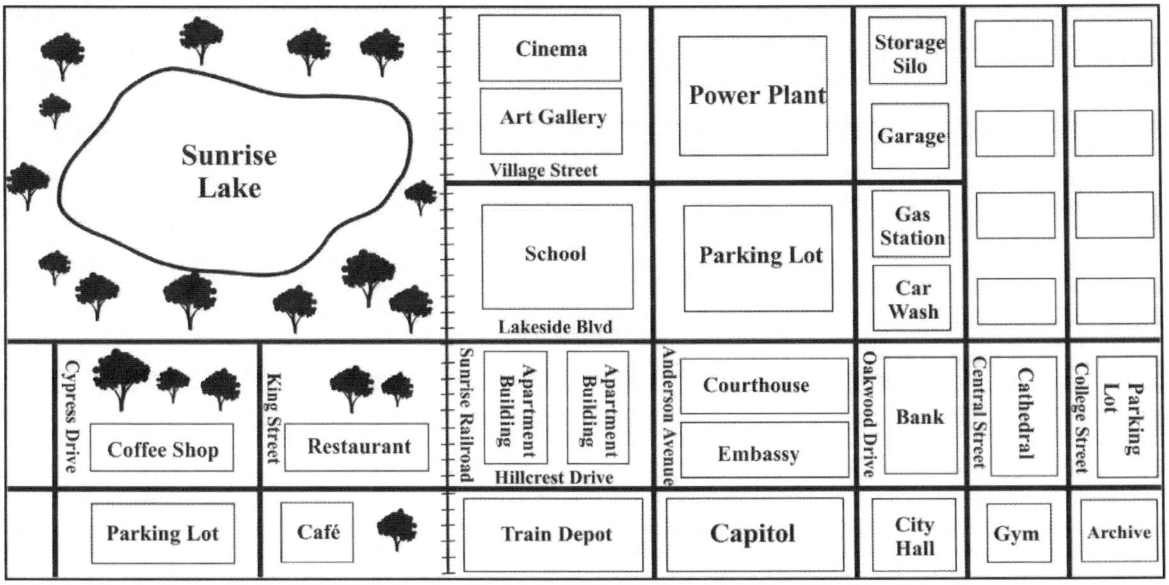

9. Patrolling on the east side of the storage silo, Officers Rowland and Bradley are dispatched to the coffee shop to investigate a broken window. Which of these is the shortest route between their location and the coffee shop?

a. Drive south on Central Street and west on Hillcrest Drive.
b. Drive south on Central Street and west on Lakeside Boulevard.
c. Drive west on Village Street and south on Anderson Avenue.
d. Drive north on Oakwood Drive and south on Hillcrest Drive.

10. If an officer needs to get from the cinema to the archive, which of these routes will involve traveling the shortest distance and the fewest turns?

a. Drive north on College Street, west on Lakeside Boulevard, and north on Anderson Avenue.
b. Drive west on Hillcrest Drive and north on Anderson Avenue.
c. Drive south on Anderson Avenue and east on Hillcrest Drive.
d. Drive west on Village Street and south on Central Street.

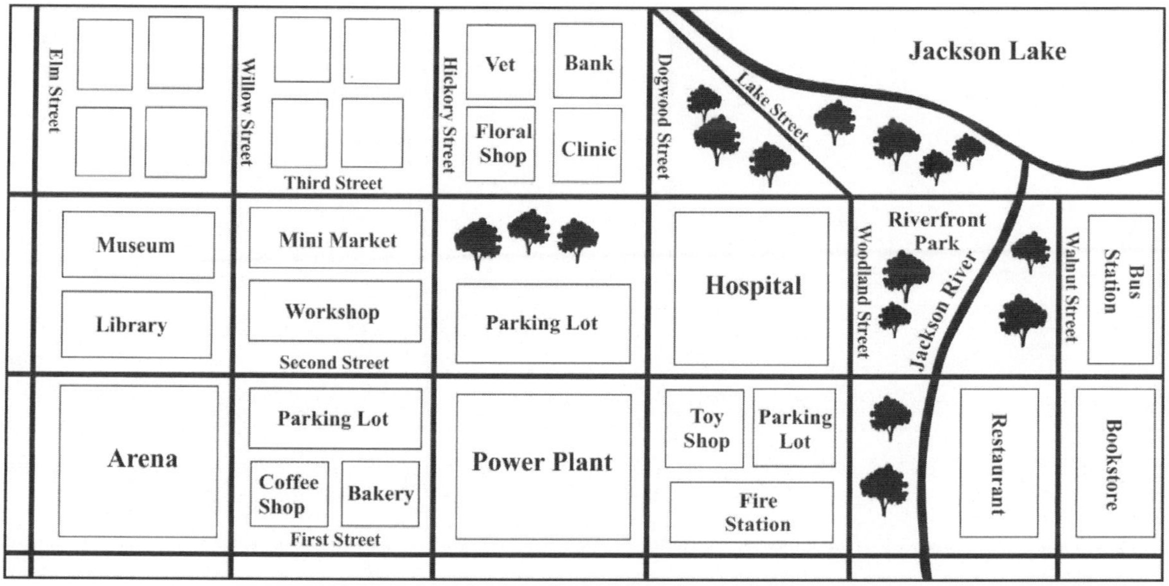

11. Two officers are at the corner of Elm and Third, and they need to get to the scene of a reported assault between the bus station and the bookstore. Which of these routes will involve traveling the shortest distance to get to the location of the reported assault?

a. Drive west on Third Street and north on Walnut Street.
b. Drive north on Walnut Street and west on Third Street.
c. Drive south on Willow Street and east on First Street.
d. Drive east on Third Street and south on Walnut Street.

12. Officer Chin is on his beat, between the arena and the coffee shop, when he receives a call about a disturbance in the wooded area between Jackson Lake and Riverfront Park. Which of these routes will involve traveling the shortest distance to get to the location of the reported disturbance?

a. Drive north on Willow Street and east on Third Street.
b. Drive south on Willow Street, east on First Street, north on Woodland Street.
c. Drive north on Willow Street, east on Second Street, north on Walnut Street, and west on Third Street.
d. Drive west on Third Street and south on Willow Street.

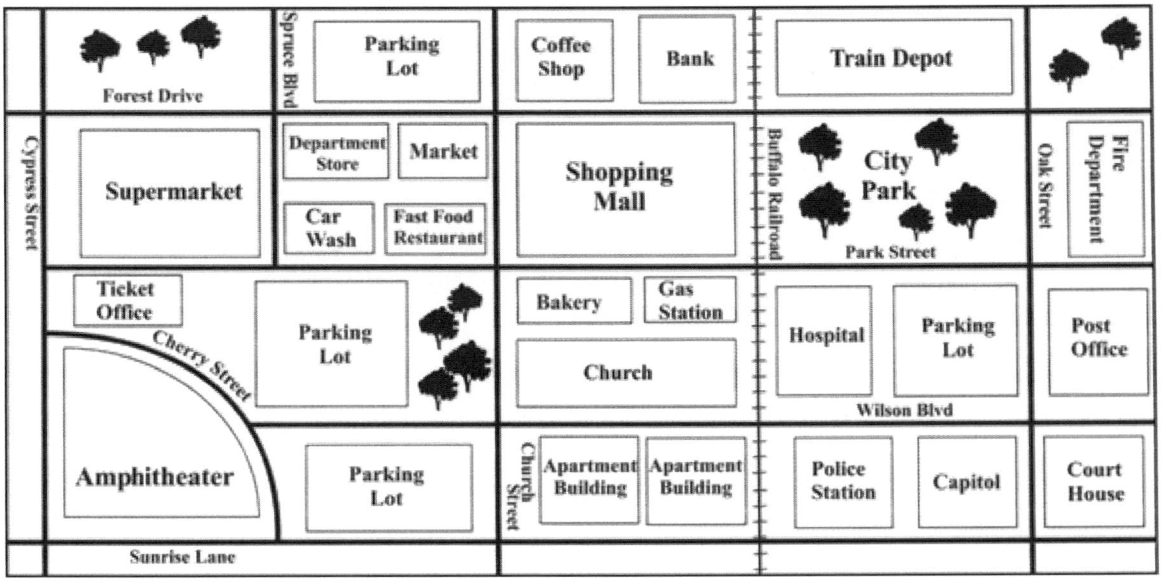

13. Officers Jensen and McDonald have been dispatched to the scene of a traffic accident between the city park and the fire department building. They are currently patrolling the area just north of the supermarket. Which of these routes will involve traveling the shortest distance as they proceed from their current location to the scene of the accident?

a. Drive north on Spruce Boulevard, east on Park Street, and south on Oak Street.
b. Drive south on Spruce Boulevard, east on Park Street, and south on Oak Street.
c. Drive south on Cypress Street, east on Park Street, and north on Oak Street.
d. Drive east on Forest Drive and south on Oak Street.

14. Officer Roberts is driving between the shopping mall and the coffee shop when he is dispatched to provide security at the courthouse for a press conference by the mayor. Which of these is the shortest route between his current location and the courthouse?

a. Drive west on Forest Drive, south on Church Street, east on Sunrise Lane, and north on Oak Street.
b. Drive east on Forest Drive and south on Oak Street.
c. Drive west on Park Street, south on Cypress Street, and east on Cherry Street.
d. Drive south on Spruce Boulevard and east on Park Street.

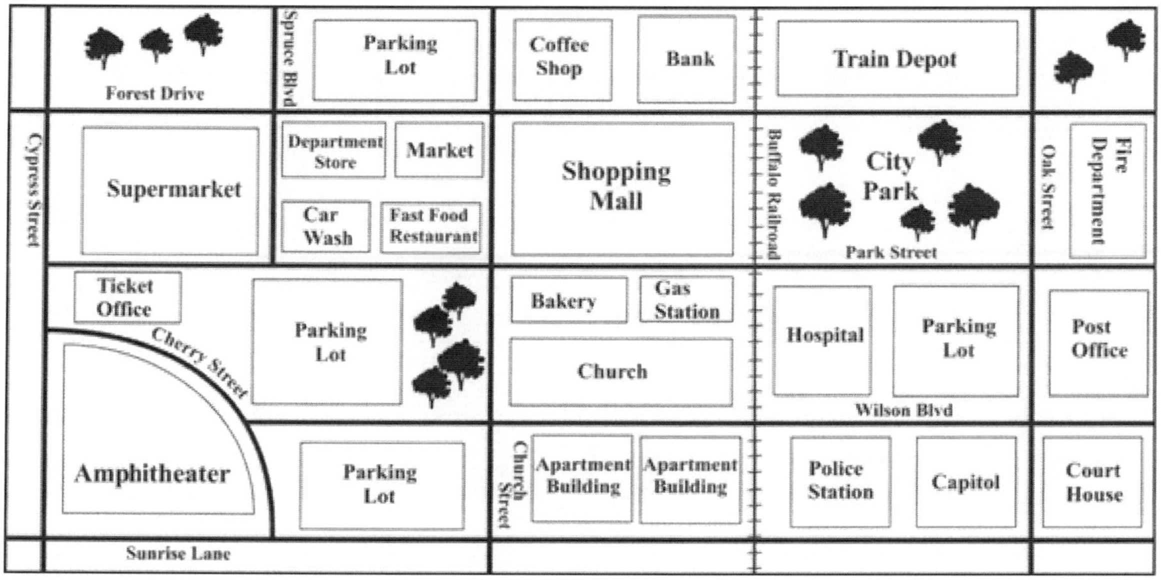

15. Officer Jefferson is parked in his patrol car between the amphitheater and the ticket office when he is dispatched to the train depot to investigate a case of vandalism. Which of these is the shortest route between his current location and the train depot?

a. Drive north on Cypress, east on Park Street, and north on Oak Street.
b. Drive southeast on Cherry Street, east on Wilson Boulevard, and north on Oak Street.
c. Drive northwest on Cherry Street, south on Cypress Street, east on Sunrise Lane, and north on Oak Street.
d. Drive southeast on Cherry Street, east on Sunrise Lane, and north on Oak Street.

Visualization

In the pictures below, which of the answer choices shows the same block as the original?

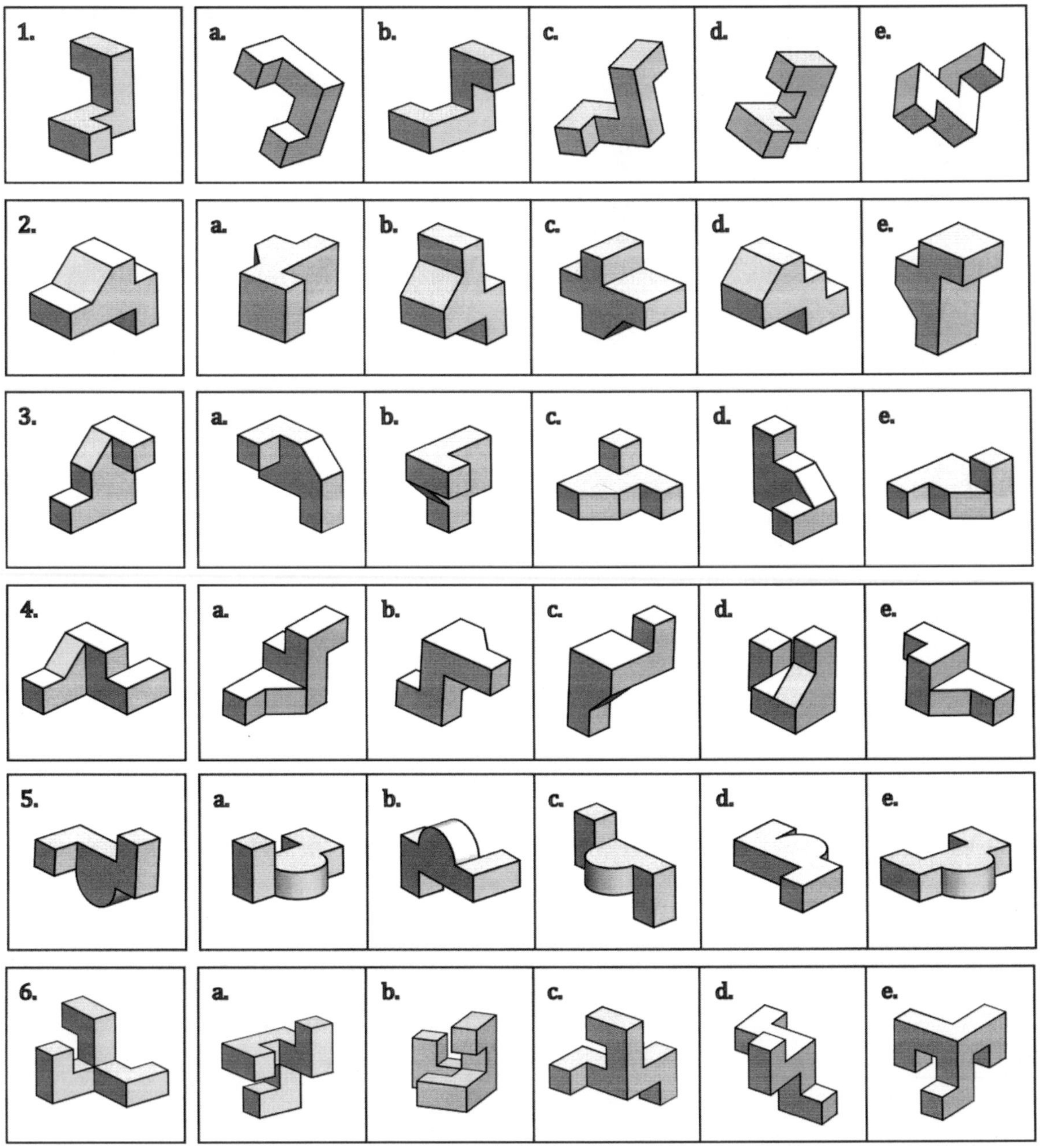

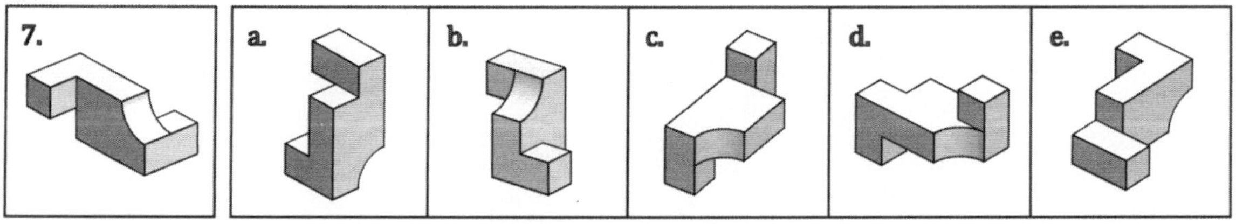

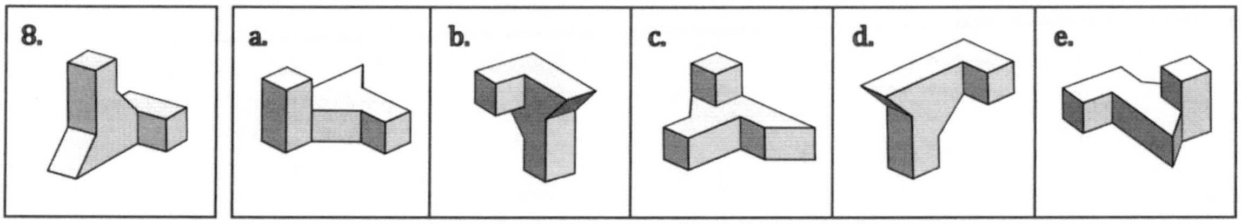

A flat square of paper is folded one or more times. The broken lines indicate the original position of the paper. The solid lines indicate the position of the folded paper. The paper is never turned or twisted. The folded paper always remains within the edges of the original square. There are multiple folds in each item. After the last fold, a hole is punched in the paper. Your task is to mentally unfold the paper and determine the position of the holes on the original square. Choose the pattern of black circles that indicates the position of the holes on the original square. There is only one correct pattern for each item.

9.

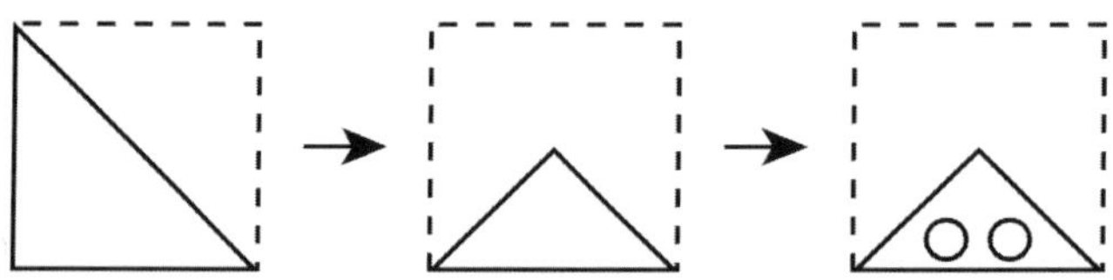

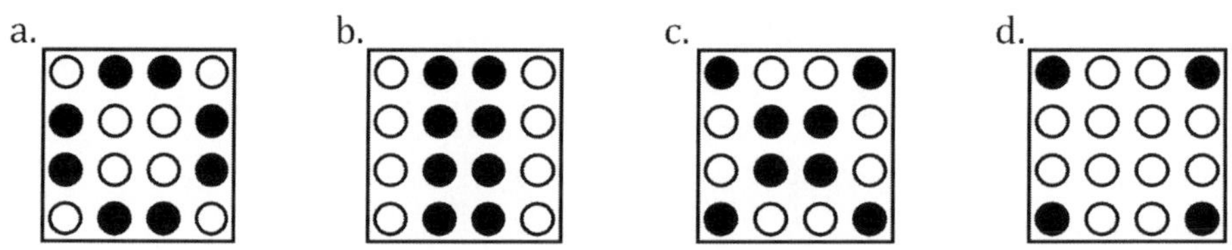

10.

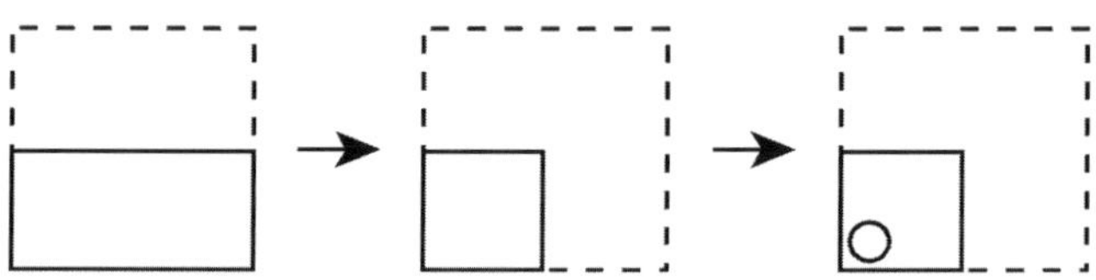

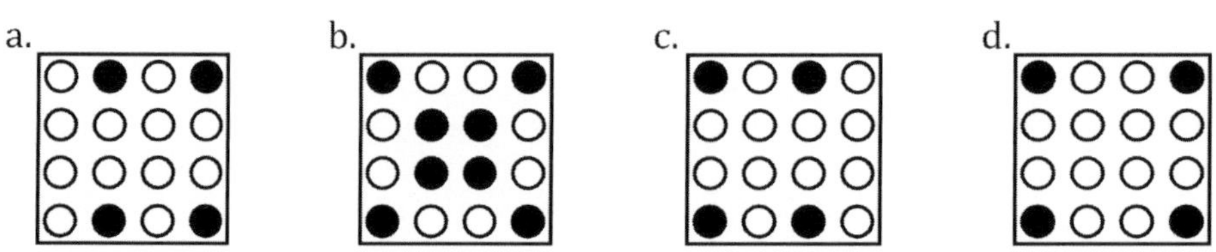

11.

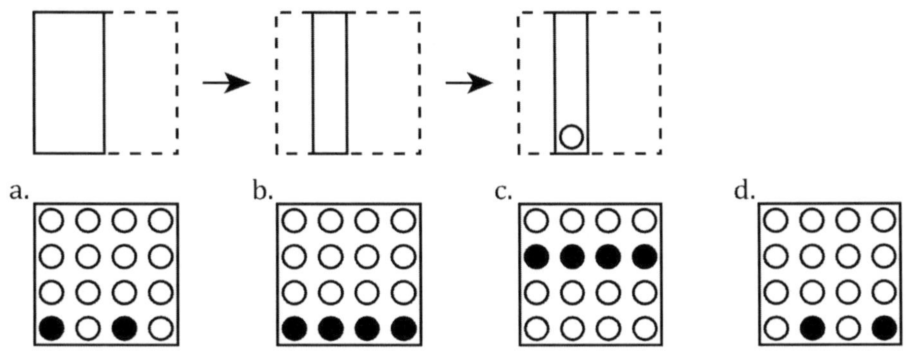

12.

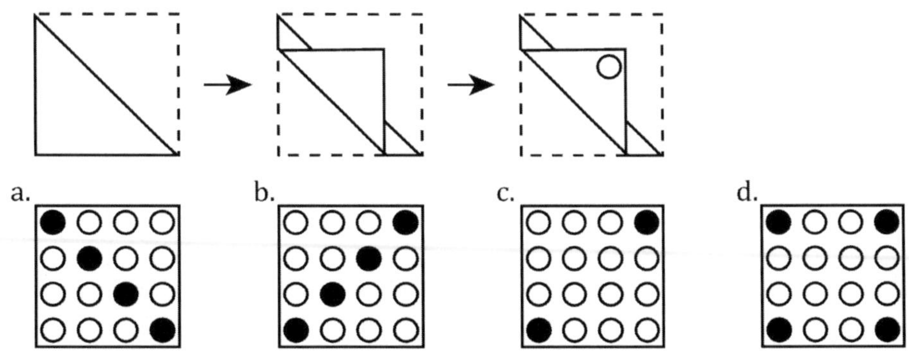

13.

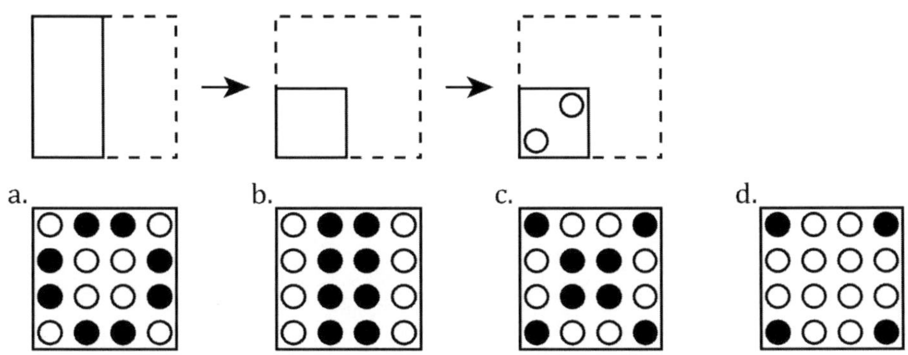

14.

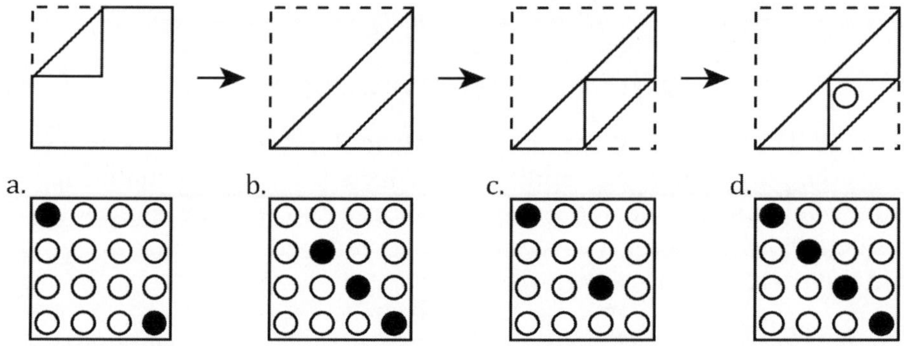

15.

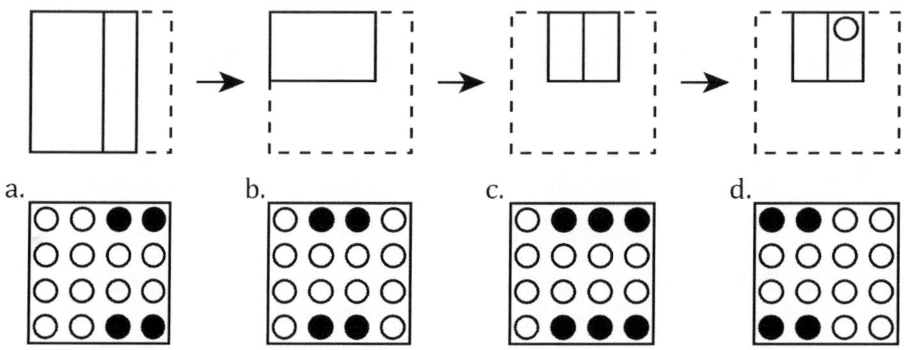

Answer Key and Explanations

Written Comprehension

1. A: Officer Shantel Williams. The passage states that Jose Mendez punched a man who spilled a drink, and that the name of the man who spilled the drink was Roland Hemphill. It goes on to say that Officer Shantel Williams interviewed Hemphill. Officer Ronald Jones interviewed Mendez. Officer Mike Smith interviewed several witnesses who confirmed Hemphill's account. Officer Mark Jones interviewed the bartender, Tyreese Smith.

2. B: Two. Asia Campos was arrested on an outstanding warrant, and Ronald Holderman was arrested for the theft of the motorcycle from Orlando.

3. C: Seven items of contraband were found in the sweep — (1) a marijuana cigarette in Inmate Reggie Wilson's pillow, (2) a cup of homemade wine in Inmate Robert Doolittle's cell, (3) a mobile phone in the cell of Inmates Mustafa Johnson and Dewayne Smith, and (4, 5, 6 and 7) three syringes and a metal spoon in a cell shared by Inmates Ryan McDonald and Brent Travers.

4. C: Seven days. Ms. Snowden checked into the hotel on June 20. She was seen on June 22, but hasn't been seen since. The date of the officer's visit is June 29, which means seven days have passed since June 22, the last time anyone saw Ms. Snowden.

5. C: 5 feet 8 inches and 150 pounds. The tallest bank robber took off going east in a brown van, the second tallest went west on a motorcycle, the short, stocky one fled west in a white Honda Civic, and the other shorter robber drove west in a small pickup truck. There were two "shorter" robbers, each about 5 feet 8 inches. But one was stockier than the other, and he drove off in a white Honda Civic. That means the robber who was 5 feet 8 inches and 150 pounds is the one who fled in a pickup truck.

6. B: Two. Although Donte Broomfield threatened four people at the pay-per-view party and assaulted another person at another house before the party, the passage states that he physically assaulted two women at the pay-per-view party.

7. B: Crews and Mason. Corrections Officer Crews was assigned to Unit B for the first and third weeks, and Unit C for the second and fourth weeks. Corrections Officer Mason was assigned to Unit B for the first and third weeks, and Unit C for the second and fourth weeks.

8. D: Wellstone. Nesmith was seen stealing a hooded sweatshirt, Jackson is seen stealing women's cosmetics, Pierson was observed stealing candy, and Nesmith was seen on tape stuffing a dress down his pants.

9. A: Five. According to the neighbor, within the last six months, police officers had been to the house to investigate (1) public intoxication, (2) another time for a domestic dispute call, (3) a few weeks later for loud music, (4) then again for cars parking illegally and impeding traffic, and (5) the last time for a person who was drunk and disorderly.

10. D: The intersection of Eldridge and Scranton. The suspect turned east onto Eldridge Avenue, and then nearly caused a collision with another car at the intersection of Scranton Street.

11. D: Ethan Jones. The passage says that Ethan Jones, the son of Eric Jones, had a makeshift bandage around his head, which was stained with blood.

12. C: Gangster Disciples. Nine members of the Mexican Mafia were moved or transferred out, six members of the outlaws were moved or transferred out, nine members of the Latin Kings were moved or transferred out, and ten members of the Gangster Disciples were moved or transferred out.

13. C: Three. The first-time officers went to the scene, they apprehended two women, who were arrested. The second time, they detained five men and three women. Of the women, two were let go, and one was arrested. Added to the two arrested previously, that makes a total of three women arrested.

14. B: Caitlyn Malcolm. Britney Maddox, Rob Tellinger, and Ryan Tellinger were all passengers in the car driven by Caitlyn Malcolm, who was arrested for DUI.

15. D: Twelve. Friday night there were three arrests for selling drugs. Saturday afternoon there were two more. Late Saturday and early Sunday yielded seven more arrests for drug sales, for a total of twelve.

Written Expression

1. A: The word *depudy* should be spelled *deputy*. The other words are spelled correctly.

2. C: The correct word to use to fill in the blank is *described*. None of the other words make any sense in this sentence. *Describe* means to give an account, or to relate facts. *Subscribe* means to receive something on a regular basis, like a cable TV subscription. *Prescribe* means to recommend something, like a doctor's prescription. *Ascribe* means to say that something is caused by something else, as in "Steve ascribed his sore knees to too much jogging yesterday."

3. B: The word *arive* should be spelled *arrive*. The other words are spelled correctly.

4. C: *Must* is the only choice for filling in the blank that follows good grammar.

5. D. The word *cittizens* should be spelled *citizens*. The other words are spelled correctly.

6. A: The word *is* is the only choice for filling in the blank that follows good grammar.

7. A: The word *funural* should be spelled *funeral*. The other words are spelled correctly.

8. B: The word *assigned* is the only choice for filling in the blank that makes sense and follows good grammar.

9. B: The word *unpleasent* should be spelled *unpleasant*. The other words are spelled correctly.

10. D: The word *be* is the only choice for filling in the blank that follows good grammar.

11. C: The word *cheif* should be spelled *chief*. The other words are spelled correctly.

12. D: The phrase *be admitted to* is the only choice for filling in the blank that follows good grammar.

13. C: The word *steap* should be spelled *steep*. The other words are spelled correctly.

14. A: The phrase *have been* is the only choice for filling in the blank that follows good grammar.

15. C: The word *endorce* should be spelled *endorse*. The other words are spelled correctly.

Memorization

1. C: There are 14 people in the photo. There are 13 on or beside the stairs, and in the background, there is a woman with her back to the camera behind the man who is next to the stairs.

2. B: One person in the front row is wearing a dress.

3. B: One person is wearing glasses—the woman the dog is standing in front of.

4. D: The woman whose luggage the dog is sniffing is reading a book.

5. D: The officer on the right is taller.

6. C: The officer on the left is wearing sunglasses.

7. D: The officer on the right is in short sleeves.

8. C: The officer on the left is wearing a cap.

9. C: The officer on the left is wearing gloves.

10. B: The officer in the middle is tallest.

11. A: The officer on the left is holding his beverage in his right hand.

12. C: The street sign says 24th St

13. A: According to the mileage sign, Condon is 38 miles away.

14. A: The mileage sign is taller.

15. B: The arrow on the road sign is pointing left.

Problem Sensitivity

1. B: Of the four choices, a man pulling a kid's wagon down the sidewalk containing four cases of beer would be the most likely case of looting. A man who can afford to purchase four cases of beer at once probably owns a car, and wouldn't be using a child's toy to transport the beer. Many people sit on their porches and listen to music, and there's nothing inherently suspicious about owning new electronic devices, so A is wrong. The same goes for urban fashion—lots of teenagers own trendy clothes which they bought and paid for. Plus, if the teenager had just stolen them, it's unlikely he would be wearing them already, so C is also wrong. The man with the expensive bicycle looks like he just finished a long ride, and he is dressed for the part, so there's no reason to think he stole the bike, making D a poor choice.

2. D: The most likely explanation for their behavior is that they were planning on breaking into the store. Their explanations either make no sense, or they contradict one another. It would be very odd to just "hang out" at midnight in front of a store at a strip mall, especially since that would be considered loitering, which is against the law, so A is wrong. Most people know that a shoe store in a strip mall is not going to be open at midnight, so B isn't believable. While it's possible that a popular new shoe is being released the next morning, that's highly unlikely to be true since it's the third story they've come up with, so C is wrong. And the fact that they told three different stories is strong evidence that none of them are true.

3. A: A driver who begins constantly switching lanes after seeing that a police car is behind him, while always being careful to signal each lane change, is exhibiting very unusual behavior. Many people change lanes without signaling; repeatedly changing lanes and signaling every single one suggests that the driver is concerned about being pulled over and he wants to get out of your line of sight, but he's also being hyper-cautious about following the letter of the law so as to not give you a reason to pull him over. A driver ahead of you who signals a right turn but changes his mind, turns his signal off, and goes straight, is obviously not trying to evade you, so the driver in C shouldn't raise any concerns. There's really nothing suspicious at all about the behavior of the drivers in B and D.

4. C: You should stop and deal with the situation and notify dispatch about the unplanned stop. It looks as if a fight is about to break out, and preventing violence takes priority over investigating a car break-in that already happened.

5. C: After the meeting, ask the supervisor to clarify what you didn't understand. Talking to your fellow officers about what the supervisor said isn't a good idea because they may have had just as much trouble hearing it as you did, or they may not remember it correctly, so A is wrong. The actions in answers B and D are irresponsible because the information you missed may well be both very important and urgent, so assuming that no major changes are required or that if they're really important you'll get an email are wrong choices.

6. A: You should order everyone out of the area and call for the bomb squad. There have been several terrorist bombings around the world using abandoned backpacks, and a full backpack that has been sitting unattended for a couple of hours near a busy parade route is highly suspicious. Under no circumstances should you touch it, let alone open it, and you should not tell the bystanders to give it a couple hours and then you'll notify your superiors.

7. D: The most likely explanation is that there is something in the car the driver doesn't want you to see. From a distance, a person under the influence of drugs might act very much like a person under the influence of alcohol, and he's not exhibiting any signs of intoxication, so A is probably not correct. It's possible the car is stolen, but it's not the most likely explanation, as the driver would probably have tried to evade you by taking off at high speed when you turned your lights on, or fleeing on foot after pulling over. So B is slightly plausible, but not the most likely explanation. C is not a good explanation, as a driver who is merely in a hurry to get somewhere would probably be very co-operative, and would be very unlikely to offer you a bribe. That leaves D as the most likely scenario.

8. B: Of the four answer choices, the most plausible is that the man bought a pack of cigarettes for the boy who is too young to buy them legally. A doesn't make much sense, as a boy would not call a stranger over and offer to loan him money out of the blue, nor would the man put the change in the bag. C is very unlikely, as the boy could've gone in and bought gum very quickly, and if his mother had shown up, she would've waited. D is also highly implausible, as a child who found a winning lotto ticket probably would get a family member to cash it for him, instead of approaching a complete stranger, and as with A, the man wouldn't put the money in his bag.

9. C: Your first priority should be helping the young adult woman who is bleeding profusely from her left arm. The teenage girl who is moaning and barely conscious needs medical attention of a higher level than you are able to provide, and nothing you can do for her will likely improve her condition, so A is wrong. An elderly woman who is ambulatory but disoriented certainly could use your help, but that is not as important as preventing a woman from bleeding to death, so B is incorrect. D is wrong because there is not much you can do to repair a broken arm. However, you

can use your skill level to save the adult woman from bleeding to death by applying your first aid knowledge to stem her bleeding.

10. D: The most likely explanation is that the man is experiencing a medical emergency, such as a heart attack, or the onset of diabetic shock. While all of the other answers are possibly true, none are the most likely scenario. Elderly people rarely abuse illegal drugs, so A is not likely. The passage doesn't say anything about injuries, so there's no support for B, that he was mugged. C is more plausible than A or B, but the fact that he is sweating profusely indicates a medical condition other than Alzheimer's.

11. B: The only really likely scenario is that the driver and passenger are involved in illegal drug use or sales and fear arrest. If a driver accelerates and a passenger tosses something out the window immediately after you turn on your flashing lights, it's pretty clear they know you want them to pull over, so A is obviously wrong. If the driver were in a hurry to get to the hospital, he would've been speeding long before you signaled him to pull over, so C is out. If the driver were looking for a safer place to pull over, there'd be no need to accelerate, or throw anything out the window, so D is extremely unlikely.

12. A: The best explanation of the four possible choices is that the truck is stolen. Mix-ups of this kind at the DMV are rare, so B is unlikely. It's also extremely unusual for a person to mix up which set of plates go on which of his vehicles, so C is also unlikely. It's also very hard to imagine how a person could confuse a fairly new pickup truck with an older sedan, so D is extremely unlikely.

13. D. Two men shouting at each other from their cars over the right to a parking space is the conversation that should most concern a law enforcement officer. A and C are the kinds of conversations that friends and family members regularly engage in, so they should be of no concern. B involves two men "arguing loudly", but the argument is over sports, and people argue about which sports team is the best all the time, and these arguments rarely escalate into violence. However, two drivers in a shouting match over a parking space could very easily turn into a violent confrontation.

14. B: The account from Witness #2 doesn't line up with the statements of the other three witnesses in important details. Witnesses #1 and #4 said the perpetrator was either a black or Hispanic male, indicating a male with a dark complexion. Witness #3 said she didn't get a good look at him, so she couldn't identify his race. So if two witnesses say he either black or Hispanic, one says she couldn't see his complexion, and another says he was white, the one who says he saw a white man is problematic. Additionally, all three of the other witnesses say the mugger was wearing a dark hoodie, while Witness #2 says he was wearing a white t-shirt. Because his statement is so radically different in these important details from the statements of the others, it's likely that he didn't actually witness the crime.

15. C: While all of the roads described may be closed at some point if the flooding continues, the highest priority is the busy two lane side road where several drivers and passengers have drowned in past floods. As it's a Sunday, the road to an industrial park is likely to have very little traffic, making A incorrect. B is a poor choice because it will take more than one police car to block it, and there's no indication that it has been especially dangerous in past floods. D is incorrect because cul-de-sacs get very little traffic; any traffic in a flood situation from a cul-de-sac would mostly be the residents trying to get away from the flood zone, not into it. The fact that several people have died on the side road in past floods means it's very dangerous, and should be top priority.

Number Facility

1. D: This is a simple addition problem. Start with the ones column (on the right). Add the figures 6+1, 3+0, 2+3 to get the answer 537.

2. A: This is a subtraction problem which involves borrowing to get the answer of 189.

$$\begin{array}{r} \\ 356 \\ -\ 167 \\ \hline \\ \end{array} \qquad \begin{array}{r} {\scriptstyle +10} \\ 346 \\ -\ 167 \\ \hline 9 \end{array} \qquad \begin{array}{r} {\scriptstyle +10+10} \\ 246 \\ -\ 167 \\ \hline 89 \end{array} \qquad \begin{array}{r} {\scriptstyle +10+10} \\ 246 \\ -\ 167 \\ \hline 189 \end{array}$$

3. B: This is a subtraction problem which also involves borrowing to get the answer of 1,819. In this case, it involves borrowing from zero, which just means that the zero needs to borrow from the next digit to become 10 and then it becomes 9 to lend to the original digit.

$$\begin{array}{r} \\ 5306 \\ -\ 3487 \\ \hline \\ \end{array} \qquad \begin{array}{r} {\scriptstyle +10} \\ 5206 \\ -\ 3487 \\ \hline \\ \end{array} \qquad \begin{array}{r} {\scriptstyle +9+10} \\ 5206 \\ -\ 3487 \\ \hline 9 \end{array} \qquad \begin{array}{r} {\scriptstyle +9+10} \\ 5206 \\ -\ 3487 \\ \hline 19 \end{array} \qquad \begin{array}{r} {\scriptstyle +10\ +9+10} \\ 4206 \\ -\ 3487 \\ \hline 819 \end{array} \qquad \begin{array}{r} {\scriptstyle +10\ +9+10} \\ 4206 \\ -\ 3487 \\ \hline 1819 \end{array}$$

4. A: This is a simple division problem. Divide the 7 into 9. It goes in 1 time. Write 1 above the 9 and subtract 7 from 9 to get 2. Bring down the 1 and place it beside the 2. Divide 7 into 21. It goes in 3 times. Divide 7 into 7. It goes 1 time.

$$\begin{array}{r} 131 \\ 7\overline{)\,917} \\ \underline{7} \\ 21 \\ \underline{21} \\ 07 \\ \underline{07} \\ 0 \end{array}$$

5. A: To change this fraction into a decimal, move the decimal to the right two places: 0.38.

6. C: This is a simple addition problem. Line up the decimals so that they are all in the same place in the equation, and see that there is a 6 by itself in the hundredth's column. Then add the tenths column: 8 + 3 = 11. Write down the 1 and carry the 1. Add the ones column: 6 + 1 plus the carried 1. Write down 8. Then write down the 1.

$$\begin{array}{r} \\ 6.8 \\ 11.3 \\ +\ 0.06 \\ \hline \\ \end{array} \qquad \begin{array}{r} {\scriptstyle +1} \\ 6.8 \\ 11.3 \\ +\ 0.06 \\ \hline 16 \end{array} \qquad \begin{array}{r} {\scriptstyle +1} \\ 6.8 \\ 11.3 \\ +\ 0.06 \\ \hline 8.16 \end{array} \qquad \begin{array}{r} {\scriptstyle +1} \\ 6.8 \\ 11.3 \\ +\ 0.06 \\ \hline 18.16 \end{array}$$

7. A: This is a subtraction problem with decimals. Be sure to line up the decimals.

$$\begin{array}{r} \\ 0.58 \\ -\ 0.39 \\ \hline \\ \end{array} \qquad \begin{array}{r} {\scriptstyle +10} \\ 0.48 \\ -\ 0.39 \\ \hline 9 \end{array} \qquad \begin{array}{r} {\scriptstyle +10} \\ 0.48 \\ -\ 0.39 \\ \hline 0.19 \end{array}$$

8. D: This is multiplication with decimals. It is often easiest to perform the multiplication on the numbers without the decimals and then figure out where to put the decimal in the final result. To do this, convert the decimals to fractions and then multiply:

$$0.25 \times 0.03 = \frac{25}{100} \times \frac{3}{100} = \frac{25 \times 3}{100 \times 100} = \frac{25 \times 3}{10000} \qquad \begin{array}{r} {}^{+1} \\ 25 \\ \times \quad 3 \\ \hline 75 \end{array} \qquad \frac{75}{10000} = 0.0075$$

9. A: To add fractions, ensure that the denominator (the number on the bottom) is the same. Since it is not, change them both to 56ths. 1/8 equals 7/56. 3/7 equals 24/56. Now add the whole numbers: $3 + 6 = 9$ and the fractions 31/56.

$$3\frac{1}{8} + 6 + \frac{3}{7} = (3 + 6) + \left(\frac{1}{8} + \frac{3}{7}\right) = (3 + 6) + \left(\frac{7}{56} + \frac{24}{56}\right) = (9) + \left(\frac{31}{56}\right) = 9\frac{31}{56}$$

10. A: To multiply mixed numbers, first create improper fractions. Multiply the whole number by the denominator, then add the numerator. $1\frac{1}{4}$ becomes $\frac{5}{4}$; $3\frac{2}{5}$ becomes $\frac{17}{5}$; $1\frac{2}{3}$ becomes $\frac{5}{3}$. Now, multiply all the numerators together and then all the denominators together:

$$\frac{5}{4} \times \frac{17}{5} \times \frac{5}{3} = \frac{5 \times 17 \times \cancel{5}}{4 \times \cancel{5} \times 3} = \frac{85}{12} = 7\frac{1}{12}$$

11. D: Recall that 'percent' means per 100. So, the fraction $\frac{36}{100}$ is the same as 36 per 100 or 36%.

12. C: 40% can be thought of as 40 per hundred. Since there are 9 hundreds in 900, then there will be 9 forties in 40% of 900: $9 \times 40 = 360$.

13. B: Rewrite the problem as 0.06*25 and solve.

14. D: Divide 4 by 16 (not 16 by 4) to get 0.25. Then move the decimal two places to the right to find the percentage.

15. C: To change a percent to a decimal, remove the percent sign and move the decimal two spaces to the left.

Mathematical Reasoning

1. C: Use approximation to solve this problem quickly: $25 \times \$3 = \$75$. The actual cost to fill the tank was $25.2 \times \$2.98 = \$75.10$.

2. C: Since one half of the wealth is being distributed in 5 equal parts, each relative is receiving $\frac{1}{5}$ of the $\frac{1}{2}$. In other words, $\frac{1}{5} \times \frac{1}{2} = \frac{1}{10}$.

3. B: In order to find the number of cans of food he gave to the first charity, the number of cans of food he has left needs to be subtracted from the number of cans he collected; $1{,}082 - 602 = 480$.

4. B: She runs 12×8 laps in all, or 96 laps.

5. C: Since he approved 13 trees out of every group of trees and surveyed 15 groups, he approved 13×15 trees, or 195 trees.

6. B: The number of cupcakes sold can be rounded as follows: 80 cupcakes, 50 cupcakes, and 70 cupcakes, which sum to 200. Therefore, the best estimate for the number of cupcakes sold is 200 cupcakes.

7. B: The amount of money Lynn has to spend on groceries for the month can be rounded to \$300; $300 \div 4 = 75$. Thus, the best estimate for the amount of money he can spend per week is \$75.

8. B: The amount of money Carlisle charges per hair cut can be rounded to \$20; $20 \times 30 = 600$. Thus, his total charges are approximately \$600.

9. B: The length of a book is possibly $11\frac{1}{2}$ inches; one-half of a meter is 50 centimeters, which would be almost 2 feet; 8 millimeters is less than 1 centimeter; and 2 yards is equal to 6 feet. None of the other measurements are likely for a book length.

10. B: A chair may possibly weigh 15 pounds; 1 ton is equal to 2,000 pounds; 3 kilograms is equal to 3,000 grams; and 6 grams is the weight of about 12 pencils.

11. B: The largest multiple of 12 less than 141 is $12 \times 11 = 132$. This leaves $141 - 132 = 9$ donuts remaining.

12. A: Use the area formula for a square: $A = s^2$. Solve the equation: $81 = s^2, s = \pm 9$. Since the side of the garden is a length, it must be positive, $s = 9$ feet.

13. B: Working the problem backwards, Jody had \$29 before she went to the movies. This was half of the money she made at the bake sale. This means $2 \times \$29 = \$58$ was made at the bake sale.

14. D: Since the marbles are being equally distributed in 4 equal parts, each friend is simply receiving $\frac{1}{4}$ of the marbles.

15. D: The other choices define A. Raising the wholesale price by \$1.75. B. Multiplying the wholesale price by 0.25 and then adding \$1.50. C. Multiplying the wholesale price by 1.75.

16. D: The approximate price of the fence is found by rounding to 70 feet at \$4 per foot. $P = 70 \times \$4 = \$280$. The actual price is $P = 71 \times \$3.98 = \$282.58$.

17. B: Performing long division gives the number of weeks and days: $145 \div 7 = 20\ R5$. The quotient 20 is the number of weeks, the remainder of 5 is the number of days.

Deductive Reasoning

1. D: She will likely not be convicted of any felony. She had \$38,000 in money from drug deals in her possession. Because that is between \$30,000 and \$150,000, ordinarily it would qualify as a third-degree felony. However, she was on her way to turn the counterfeit money over to the closest law enforcement authority, the county sheriff. According to section (b) of the quoted portion of the criminal code, if a person has the money in their possession because they are acting with intent to facilitate the lawful seizure of illicit money, that is a defense from prosecution.

2. C: Quit the team immediately. Rule 29 says: "Associating or fraternizing with any person known to have been convicted of any felony or misdemeanor, either State or Federal, excluding traffic and municipal ordinance violations." It does not mention any exceptions, so the fact that your teammate has turned his life around in the five years since getting out of prison is meaningless as far as the rule is concerned, so *A* is wrong. Only associating with him at games still violates the rule,

which doesn't allow for any fraternization or association, so *B* is incorrect. *D* is wrong because there's nothing to talk over with your supervisor, as the rule is clear and you should never ask for permission to break an official rule.

3. B: An inmate burning his arm with a lit cigarette. There is nothing in the information listed that would indicate that an inmate caught smoking a cigarette, smoking a joint, or possessing a cellphone would not be punished, so *A, C,* and *D* are all incorrect. However, (4) says that "commission of acts that should normally result in consideration for formal disciplinary action shall not be subject to such action when these acts are directly associated with an inmate's intentional self-injurious behavior," so even if it's violation of the rules for an inmate to possess a cigarette, the inmate should not be punished for trying to harm himself, but should instead receive the medical or psychological help he obviously needs.

4. B: (g). She would be in violation of the rule in (g) that says that hair dye must be a natural color. Since no humans have blue hair naturally, her blue highlights are forbidden. (f) is about neckties, so it isn't the right answer. (h) says that earrings are prohibited for male employees, but female employees are allowed to wear them. (j) is a broad rule about avoiding eccentricities and doesn't apply in this case.

5. A: While there are some rules that apply to children of different ages, (3) says "Visitors shall be required to register for visiting through the automated visiting record. The failure to do so or providing false information shall result in denial or termination of the visit and suspension of visiting privileges." Because no exceptions are listed, this applies to all child visitors, no matter their age.

6. D: Roman candles fall under the definition of illegal fireworks, while the text says that trick matches, party poppers, and toy guns are NOT classified as illegal fireworks.

7. B: The woman has committed a third-degree felony. It is very dangerous for children to be playing in the street, and it's even worse that they're doing so when they should be in bed, so the woman has clearly committed some form of child abuse. Misdemeanor child abuse is not listed as an option, so *A* is incorrect. Likewise, first-degree felony child abuse is also not mentioned, so *D* is wrong. It would be a second-degree felony if one or both of the children had suffered "great bodily harm, permanent disability, or permanent disfigurement" as a result of their mother being negligent by letting them play in the street, but both children look healthy and have no injuries, so *C* is also incorrect.

8. C: A first-degree misdemeanor is treated as a third-degree felony. Gang-related offenses move up one degree from what the crime would be treated as if it weren't gang related. The next step up after a first-degree misdemeanor is a third-degree felony, as the text says.

9. B: Giving the man a warning about parking in handicapped parking spaces without a permit is not an acceptable response according to the guidelines, which state that the officer "shall" cite the driver for parking in a handicapped space without the required permit. So letting the driver off with a warning would be a violation of the guidelines. All three of the other answer choices would be acceptable. Note that the officer may, but isn't required to, have the car towed or charge the driver with resisting an officer without violence for not producing the permit. These two options are at the officer's discretion, but having the vehicle moved (by the driver or a city tow truck) and writing a ticket are both required actions.

10. A: The first thing you should do is call for an ambulance. If the other driver were bleeding, rendering first aid might be the first priority, but with no bleeding and no obvious injuries, there is

little someone who isn't a medical professional can do, so *B* is wrong. However, the driver clearly needs medical attention, so you should call for an ambulance immediately. *C* is incorrect because calling for an ambulance is a much higher priority than calling for a supervisor to come to the scene. *D* is wrong because the text says that cars should be allowed to remain where they are except in emergency situations. So not only should you not move the vehicles before calling an ambulance, you shouldn't move them at all.

11. C: He should be charged with theft. Even though he entered the house with the intention of stealing something, he didn't commit burglary, because burglary is entering a building without permission for the purpose of committing a crime. The homeowners invited him in, so *B* is wrong. *A* is wrong for two reasons. One, he wasn't merely only the property; he stole something. Two, like burglary, criminal trespass only occurs when someone is on or in a property without permission, and he had permission to be in the house. And because he was invited in, and didn't force his way into an occupied dwelling, it wasn't a home invasion, so *D* is wrong.

12. A: He should be charged with criminal trespass. He didn't force his way in, and the house was empty, meaning it wasn't a home invasion, so *D* is incorrect. He didn't steal anything, so *C* (theft) is also incorrect. *B* is wrong because he didn't enter the home for the purpose of committing a crime, which is the definition of burglary.

13. D: They should be charged with home invasion and theft. The key here is that the house was occupied at the time, and they forced their way in for the purpose of committing the felony of threatening bodily harm to Steve, which constitutes assault. On top of that, they stole some tools, which is theft. It's not criminal trespass (*A*), because it was an occupied dwelling they broke into. It's not burglary (*B*), for the same reason. A person who breaks into an empty house and steals something is guilty of burglary, but a person who breaks into an occupied house and steals something is guilty of home invasion. Charging them with only theft (*C*) is insufficient, because it ignores the fact that they forced themselves into an occupied dwelling.

14. D: You should order the person using the foul language to leave the area or face arrest for disorderly conduct. The guidelines say that people should only be arrested for minor incidents as a last resort, and that you should strive to keep things from escalating. If you were only dealing with one person, and not with a large and angry crowd, an arrest for disorderly conduct would be appropriate. But with a large crowd of angry workers, an arrest might cause things to escalate, so *A* is wrong. B is wrong because you are not to offer your opinion about the dispute or take sides. *C* is incorrect for the same reason.

15. C: Make no arrests and call for backup, and when enough officers are on the scene arrest the worker for the property damage. *A* is incorrect, because, while it's true that you can't take sides in the dispute, you are required to enforce the law, and willfully damaging property is illegal. *B* is wrong, because the guidelines say to arrest the offender once enough officers are on the scene to control the situation. *D* is wrong because the crowd is large and hostile, and they are threatening that there will be trouble if you arrest the worker. To make an arrest before backup officers arrive would be putting yourself, your partner, and others in serious danger.

Inductive Reasoning

1. A: The bar with the lighter shading represents the data for the city that didn't pass the law. For each year, the first bar shows the percentage of victims who *refused* to testify. The question is asking you to determine in which two years the highest percentage of victims *agreed* to testify. This is the opposite of what the graph shows, so instead of looking for the tallest two bars in this

category, you need to find the shortest two bars. In the category of victims who refused to testify in the city that didn't pass the law, the two shortest bars are in 2005 and 2007. In 2005, 25% of victims refused to testify, so 75% agreed to testify. In 2007, 15% of victims refused to testify, meaning 85% agreed to testify.

2. D: This is a very basic pie chart, and it doesn't just shade each portion of the chart, but also includes the percentages. To answer this question, you simply need to find the month with the biggest number on the chart, which is December, at 17%.

3. D: In 2013, there were a little over 2000 robberies, while there were well under 2000 auto thefts. For every other year, the number of auto thefts is higher than the number of robberies.

4. A: Only two categories increased from 2011 to 2014. The biggest category, *Non-family*, decreased from 56% to 46%. *Other Family* stayed the same at 18%. The category of abusers in the *Parent* category increased from 14% to 16, while Spouse/Partner saw an increase from 12% to 20%.

5. A: Of the five categories represented in the pie charts, only one shows the same percentage in both 2010 and 2011—Asia, at 15%.

6 B: An intersection must have a number of 1.25 or higher in the Red-Light Runners Column, *and* a number of 1.10 or higher in the Red-Light Running Accidents Column. Intersections 2, 4, and 6 all have 1.25 or higher in the Red-Light Runners Column, but 2 only has 1.00 in the Red-Light Running Accidents Column. Only intersections 4 and 6 meet both criteria—.

7 C: To answer this question, you'll need to do some math. First, convert the average times into seconds. There are sixty seconds in a minute, so 10:07 becomes 607 seconds, 9:40 is 580, 9:37 is 577, and 9:46 is 586. Adding these together gives you 2350 seconds. Divide by four to get the average, which is 587.5. Then divide 587.5 by 60 to convert it back into minutes, which produces 9, with a remainder of 47.5. So the average response time for the patrol cars in the trial was 9:47.5 seconds. This is 12.5 seconds lower than the benchmark of 10:00.

8 D: June and August both had 12 accidents. None of the other pairs had the same number of accidents. January had 10 and September had 9, making *A* wrong. February had 11 and June had 10, so *B* is wrong. May had 8 and November had 5, so *C* is incorrect.

9. B: To find the percentage difference, subtract the lower number from the higher number, and divide the result by the higher number. So in Q1 subtract 12-10 leaves 2. 2/12 is .1666, or around 17%. In other words, there were 17% more contraband items discovered at one facility than at the other for Q1. For Q3, the difference was also about 17%, while in Q4 the difference was 33%. In Q2, however, the difference was 75%.

10. D: While no two of the descriptions are exactly the same, the first three are similar enough that it's very likely they're describing the same person. In all three the suspect is white, and all three of the first victims said he is six feet tall or within a couple inches of six feet. Two of the victims say he had or might have had a tattoo on one of his arms, while the first victim doesn't remember. They all place him in about the same age range, from 25-30, although expressed in different ways. In the fourth robbery, the suspect shares the age and race of the suspect in the other three robberies, but he's described as being nearly half a foot shorter than six feet tall, and he also has a large scar on his face. It's very unlikely that this is the same suspect as in the other three muggings, because it's difficult to believe the other three victims wouldn't have noticed the scar, or would have overestimated the suspect's height so badly.

11. C: The question was which age bracket was third highest. The age bracket of 21-25 has the highest percentage of people who have driven under the influence of alcohol in the past 12 months, 23.4%. Second highest is 26-29, at 19.3%. The third highest is 30-34, at 18.0%.

12. C: The green line at the bottom of the chart represents 12- and 13-year-olds who reported that they had used alcohol in the past 30 days, and the triangle marks the year. In 2003, 4.5+% of 12- and 13-year-olds reported using alcohol in the past 30 days, and 4.5+ is the highest number on that line.

13. A: To answer this question, you can use the same formula used to answer Question 9. To find the percentage difference, subtract the lower number from the higher number, and divide the result by the higher number. Doing so will show that Irving had the greatest percentage drop of all four cities. However, it's really not necessary to do any math to find the answer. You can compare the 2012 bar to the 2013 bar with a quick glance, and see that the decrease appears to be the biggest on the city of Irving's bars, proportionally.

14. C: At Dalton, 34% of officers are white. Asian-Americans make up 4% of the staff, and Hispanics are 30%, equaling 34%.

15. B: Ferguson. Add up the percentages of officers in each age range. The facility with the highest total percentage is the facility with the greatest number of officers that need to lose weight. 44% of Milton officers, 82% of Ferguson officers, 78% of Dalton officers, and 66% of Howard officers need to lose weight.

Information Ordering

1. D: The correct sequence is 3,5,4,1,2. 3) Take a seat in a nearby chair, and place the baby face down on your forearm, which is supported by your thigh. 5) Using the heel of your hand, thump the baby firmly (but gently) in the middle of its back, five times in a row. This should dislodge the food. 4) If the back thumps don't work, then, using your forearm, hold the baby face up, head lower than trunk, and placing your fingers at the center of the breastbone, give five short chest compressions. 1) If back thumps and chest compressions have both failed, call 911. 2) While waiting for emergency responders, begin infant CPR.

2. A: The correct order is 5,1,4,2,3. 5) I was walking down the street minding my own business. 1) A man came out of an alley with a gun and demanded my wallet. 4) I gave him my wallet. 2) He struck me in the head with the butt of his gun and then took off running. 3) I didn't have my phone with me, so I asked a passerby to call the police and report the crime.

3. B: The correct order is 3,4,2,1,5. 3) Security alerted me that a person with a history of shoplifting had entered the store. 4) I went to our CCTV room and watched him as he put several items of men's clothing in his cart. 2) He left the clothing department and proceeded to the toy department and loaded several expensive toys into his cart. 1) With his cart full, he left the store without paying. 5) Two security guards apprehended him in the parking lot and detained him, and I called for your assistance.

4. D: Your next step is to ask dispatch to send a hostage negotiator and additional officers. Before attempting to establish communications with the man, you need to request a hostage negotiator and additional officers to help you cover the ground floor exists, and keep at bay any curious pedestrians or neighbors who may show up.

5. B: You're in the Empathy stage—you're trying to put yourself in the suspect's shoes in order to show him that you understand what he's going through. If you're successful, this will enable you to create Rapport with the suspect, which is the next stage.

6. B: According to the protocols set out in the question, the first thing you should do in a situation like this is to identify yourself and your law enforcement agency.

7. B: Step 2. In this step, the Firearms Inspector is to pull the trigger to make sure it's functioning properly. If it isn't, the Inspector may not proceed to Step 3, but must send the weapon to the department firing range to be examined by an armorer.

8. C: The correct order is 2,3,5,4,1. 2) Obtain official approval before using the MCC. 3) Fill out the sign-out log form in full before starting up the MCC and leaving the facility. 5) Notify Tactical Fleet Unit when the MCC is powered up on location. 4) Notify Tactical Fleet Unit when the MCC is no longer needed and on its way back to the hangar. 1) Complete Form 362, documenting any damage the MCC sustained while in operation.

9. C: The correct order is 4,1,3,5,2. 4) The first supervisor to arrive on the scene will take command. 1) He or she will then examine the body, and interview the officer or officers who were first on the scene. 3) After getting the basic information from the officers, the supervisor will make sure that no one else enters the scene until the Homicide Unit arrives. 5) After the Homicide Unit arrives, the supervisor will then assign an officer to complete Form 95, logging all information about any personnel allowed to enter the crime scene, the time of their entrance, the reason they were approved for entry, and the time they left the scene. 2) The supervisor will either remain on the crime scene until the Homicide Unit has finished processing the scene, or he or she will designate another supervisor to take command before leaving the scene.

10. A: The correct order is 2,5,1,4,3. 2) Weigh the pills before bagging. 5) Put the pills in an official evidence bag. 1) Seal the bag and weigh it. 4) On the outside of the bag, write the number of pills, the weight before bagging, and the weight including the bag. 3) After weight and count are written on the bag, mark the bag with the names and badge numbers of both the officer and the supervisor.

11. C: The correct order is 2,1,3,5,4. 2) Notify the Officer-in-Charge of the location of the day's work site and request a Road Squad van. 1) Make sure the Road Squad van is inspected for contraband and that it is both safe and mechanically reliable before any inmates are loaded. 3) Assign an officer to drive the inspected Road Squad van to the inmate pickup area. 5) Make sure that each inmate assigned to the Road Squad is completely searched before leaving the facility to enter the Road Squad van. 4) Conduct a head count and roll call before leaving the work site to return to the facility.

12. C: The correct order is 2,4,3,1,5. 2) Run the vehicle's license plate and vehicle identification numbers through the system to find the owner. 4) Attempt to contact the owner to tell them to move the vehicle. If unsuccessful, proceed to next step. 3) Mark the tires to start the 48 hour window the owner has to move the vehicle. 1) When 48 hours have passed, attach an Abandoned Vehicle Sticker (AVS) to the driver's side window. 5) Enter the AVS serial number into the Abandoned Vehicle Log.

13. D: The correct order is 3,4,2,5,1. 3) Double check every False Alarm Report for completeness and accuracy as soon as received. 4) Compare the False Alarm Report with the official computerized summary of alarm runs from the ECC. 2) Amend the False Alarm Report record as necessary to match the ECC summary. 5) Enter the information from the False Alarm Report into the alarm

billing system database. 1) Send a bill to the homeowner or business owner for the false alarm as authorized by City Ordinance 10-5927.

14. C: Step 3 says that the ECC will post the declaration on social media. Answer choice C is the only answer choice which has Step 3 in the third position.

15. A: The correct order is 4,2,5,1,3. 4) Notify all essential personnel in all sections, districts, and units, using both radio and teletype, that a Spontaneous Alert is in effect. 2) Notify all non-essential personnel on the Spontaneous Alert notification list. 5) Order all officers on routine runs to cancel their runs and await further instructions. 1) In the Computer Dispatch System (CDS) display, highlight each Hostile Area as reports of hostilities come in. 3) Dispatch cars to a Hostile Area only when requested by the Officer-in-Charge of that Hostile Area.

Spatial Orientation

1. D: Drive west on Magnolia Street, south on Spring Road, west on Clark Road, south on Taylor Road, and west on Adams Street. *A* is incorrect because the first step is to drive south on Spring Road, and since Officer Chavez is on Magnolia Street, two intersections down from Spring, it's impossible for that to be the first step. *B* is wrong for the same reason—the first step is driving west on Clark Road, which is impossible, because Officer Chavez's first action can only be to drive east or west on Magnolia Street. *C* is wrong because after driving west on Magnolia, the next steps are to drive south on Taylor Road, east on Madison Boulevard, and South on Spring Road. But this is unnecessary and involves too much travel, as Spring Road comes before Taylor Road when you're traveling west on Magnolia, and Officer Chavez should simply go South on Spring Road instead of traveling too far and then doubling back.

2. C: Drive east on Madison Boulevard, south on Spring Road, and east on Jefferson Street. *A* is wrong because the first step is driving north, and the art gallery is south of the Post Office and library. *B* is incorrect because the first step is driving west, and the art gallery is east of the Post Office and library. D is wrong because it involves turning east on Adams Street from Spring Road, but you can only go west on Adams from Spring Road, and Adams is a block south of the Art Gallery on Jefferson, so that would involve even more unnecessary travel.

3. B: Drive west on Adams Street, north on Spring Road, west on Jefferson Street, south on Taylor Road, and west on Adams Street. *A* is incorrect because going north on Spring Road and west on Magnolia will take you nowhere near the bus station, and going south on Clark Road is impossible because it runs east and west. *B* and *C* are both wrong for several reasons; including the fact that each of them begins by traveling east, when the bus station is directly west of the archive.

4. B: Drive north on Brown Street, east on Robin Street, and south on Green Street. *A* is incorrect; those directions will get the officers to the toy store, but they are not the most direct route because Hemlock Drive doesn't connect to Green Street, so they would have to turn south, turn east, and then double back by heading north on Green Street. *C* is wrong; these are actually the reverse directions, from the toy store to the eatery. *D* is wrong because the first step is driving east on Hemlock Drive, but the officers could only start driving on Brown Street, Robin Street, or Eagle Street.

5. A: Drive west on Robin Street and south on Evergreen Drive. *B* is incorrect because driving east on Robin Street is the wrong direction, and will not lead to Evergreen Drive. *C* is wrong because it begins on Fairview Drive, which isn't near the taxi station so it can't be the first step, and it doesn't end at the fire station. *D* is also incorrect; these are the reverse directions.

6. C: Drive north on Eagle Street and west on Hemlock Drive. *A* is wrong because driving South on Fairview Boulevard doesn't lead to Robin Street. *B* is incorrect because it adds an additional block to the driving distance by starting on Fairview Boulevard instead of Eagle Street. *D* is wrong because it has the officers driving north on Walker Street which runs east to west, and west on Evergreen Drive, which runs north and south.

7. B: Drive west on Shady Road and west on Grandview Drive. *A* is incorrect because Second Street is nowhere near the library where the officers are parked. *C* is wrong because the officers are on Shady Road, and there's no need to turn south onto Fourth Street only to turn around and go north on Fourth Street. *D* is wrong because if the officers follow that route, they'll end up on the south side of the plant, and they need to be on the north side.

8. C: Drive west on Shady Road, south on Fourth Street, and west on Hawthorne Street. *A* is incorrect because the first step is driving east on Hawthorne Street, but that is nowhere near Hamilton Park and it's also going in the wrong direction. The directions in *C* will get the officer there, but it adds an unnecessary turn. *D* is wrong because going northwest on Grandview Drive takes Officer Johnson further away from the hospital, not closer.

9. A: Drive south on Central Street and west on Hillcrest Drive. *B* is wrong because if the officers follow that route, they will arrive at the wooded area north of the coffee shop, instead of at the shop itself. *C* is wrong because the last step involves going south on Anderson Avenue, which is several blocks away from the coffee shop. *D* is wrong because the officers can't start on Oakwood Avenue, they wouldn't want to go north on it, and they can't go south on Hillcrest Drive because it runs east and west.

10. C: Drive south on Anderson Avenue and east on Hillcrest Drive. *A* is incorrect because these are the reverse directions, with some added distance thrown in. *B* is wrong because the cinema is nowhere near Hillcrest Drive so it would be impossible to start there, and the last step is going north on Anderson Avenue, which would take the officer far from the archive, and in the opposite direction. *D* is incorrect because going west on Village Street is the wrong direction, and would not take the officer to Central Street.

11. D: Drive east on Third Street and south on Walnut Street. *A* is incorrect because if the officers go west on Third Street, they will never reach Walnut Street, as it is east of where they are. Also, it has them going north on Walnut, when the location of the reported assault is south of them. *B* is wrong because these are actually the reverse directions. *C* is incorrect because it starts on Willow Street, but the officers can only start driving on either Elm Street or Third Street. In addition, going all the way to First Street before heading east would be rather out of the way.

12. A: Drive north on Willow Street and east on Third Street. *B* is wrong because it has Officer Chin driving south on Willow Street, when he needs to go north. *C* is incorrect because there's no need to go as far east as Walnut Street—that's too far, and the officer would have to double back. *D* is wrong, as these are the reverse directions.

13. D: Drive east on Forest Drive and south on Oak Street. *A* is wrong because going north on Spruce Boulevard is the wrong direction, and it also doesn't connect to Oak Street, but runs parallel. *B* is wrong because it adds unnecessary driving by having the officers go south on Spruce Boulevard, which takes them too far south, and would require them to head north once they got to Oak Street. *C* is wrong for the same reason—there's simply no need for the officers to drive further than necessary by heading south on Cypress Street when they can proceed straight to the location by heading east on Forest Drive.

14. B: Drive east on Forest Drive and south on Oak Street. *A* is wrong because traveling west on Forest Drive means going away from the new location, requiring a lot of extra driving to reach the courthouse. *C* is wrong because the first step is driving west on Park Street, and not only is this the wrong direction, the officer is on Forest Drive so he can't start by driving on Park Street. D is incorrect because it ends at the intersection of Oak Street and Park Street, which isn't the location of the courthouse, but is a block north of the courthouse.

15. B: Drive southeast on Cherry Street, east on Wilson Boulevard, and north on Oak Street. *A* is the wrong answer because it takes Officer Jefferson too far north by having him take Cypress Street to Forest Drive; if it had him turning east at Park Street instead of Cypress, this route would be the shortest. *C* is incorrect because Officer Jefferson would go south on Cypress Street, but the train depot is north. *D* is wrong because instead of going east on Wilson Boulevard, Officer Jefferson would have to drive all the way south to Sunrise Lane before heading north on Oak Street, and this adds unnecessary distance to the trip.

Visualization

1. C

2. E

3. D

4. B

5. A

6. C

7. D

8. A

9. A

10. D

11. B

12. C

13. C

14. D

15. A

How to Overcome Test Anxiety

Just the thought of taking a test is enough to make most people a little nervous. A test is an important event that can have a long-term impact on your future, so it's important to take it seriously and it's natural to feel anxious about performing well. But just because anxiety is normal, that doesn't mean that it's helpful in test taking, or that you should simply accept it as part of your life. Anxiety can have a variety of effects. These effects can be mild, like making you feel slightly nervous, or severe, like blocking your ability to focus or remember even a simple detail.

If you experience test anxiety—whether severe or mild—it's important to know how to beat it. To discover this, first you need to understand what causes test anxiety.

Causes of Test Anxiety

While we often think of anxiety as an uncontrollable emotional state, it can actually be caused by simple, practical things. One of the most common causes of test anxiety is that a person does not feel adequately prepared for their test. This feeling can be the result of many different issues such as poor study habits or lack of organization, but the most common culprit is time management. Starting to study too late, failing to organize your study time to cover all of the material, or being distracted while you study will mean that you're not well prepared for the test. This may lead to cramming the night before, which will cause you to be physically and mentally exhausted for the test. Poor time management also contributes to feelings of stress, fear, and hopelessness as you realize you are not well prepared but don't know what to do about it.

Other times, test anxiety is not related to your preparation for the test but comes from unresolved fear. This may be a past failure on a test, or poor performance on tests in general. It may come from comparing yourself to others who seem to be performing better or from the stress of living up to expectations. Anxiety may be driven by fears of the future—how failure on this test would affect your educational and career goals. These fears are often completely irrational, but they can still negatively impact your test performance.

Elements of Test Anxiety

As mentioned earlier, test anxiety is considered to be an emotional state, but it has physical and mental components as well. Sometimes you may not even realize that you are suffering from test anxiety until you notice the physical symptoms. These can include trembling hands, rapid heartbeat, sweating, nausea, and tense muscles. Extreme anxiety may lead to fainting or vomiting. Obviously, any of these symptoms can have a negative impact on testing. It is important to recognize them as soon as they begin to occur so that you can address the problem before it damages your performance.

The mental components of test anxiety include trouble focusing and inability to remember learned information. During a test, your mind is on high alert, which can help you recall information and stay focused for an extended period of time. However, anxiety interferes with your mind's natural processes, causing you to blank out, even on the questions you know well. The strain of testing during anxiety makes it difficult to stay focused, especially on a test that may take several hours. Extreme anxiety can take a huge mental toll, making it difficult not only to recall test information but even to understand the test questions or pull your thoughts together.

Effects of Test Anxiety

Test anxiety is like a disease—if left untreated, it will get progressively worse. Anxiety leads to poor performance, and this reinforces the feelings of fear and failure, which in turn lead to poor performances on subsequent tests. It can grow from a mild nervousness to a crippling condition. If allowed to progress, test anxiety can have a big impact on your schooling, and consequently on your future.

Test anxiety can spread to other parts of your life. Anxiety on tests can become anxiety in any stressful situation, and blanking on a test can turn into panicking in a job situation. But fortunately, you don't have to let anxiety rule your testing and determine your grades. There are a number of relatively simple steps you can take to move past anxiety and function normally on a test and in the rest of life.

Physical Steps for Beating Test Anxiety

While test anxiety is a serious problem, the good news is that it can be overcome. It doesn't have to control your ability to think and remember information. While it may take time, you can begin taking steps today to beat anxiety.

Just as your first hint that you may be struggling with anxiety comes from the physical symptoms, the first step to treating it is also physical. Rest is crucial for having a clear, strong mind. If you are tired, it is much easier to give in to anxiety. But if you establish good sleep habits, your body and mind will be ready to perform optimally, without the strain of exhaustion. Additionally, sleeping well helps you to retain information better, so you're more likely to recall the answers when you see the test questions.

Getting good sleep means more than going to bed on time. It's important to allow your brain time to relax. Take study breaks from time to time so it doesn't get overworked, and don't study right before bed. Take time to rest your mind before trying to rest your body, or you may find it difficult to fall asleep.

Along with sleep, other aspects of physical health are important in preparing for a test. Good nutrition is vital for good brain function. Sugary foods and drinks may give a burst of energy but this burst is followed by a crash, both physically and emotionally. Instead, fuel your body with protein and vitamin-rich foods.

Also, drink plenty of water. Dehydration can lead to headaches and exhaustion, especially if your brain is already under stress from the rigors of the test. Particularly if your test is a long one, drink water during the breaks. And if possible, take an energy-boosting snack to eat between sections.

Along with sleep and diet, a third important part of physical health is exercise. Maintaining a steady workout schedule is helpful, but even taking 5-minute study breaks to walk can help get your blood pumping faster and clear your head. Exercise also releases endorphins, which contribute to a positive feeling and can help combat test anxiety.

When you nurture your physical health, you are also contributing to your mental health. If your body is healthy, your mind is much more likely to be healthy as well. So take time to rest, nourish your body with healthy food and water, and get moving as much as possible. Taking these physical steps will make you stronger and more able to take the mental steps necessary to overcome test anxiety.

Mental Steps for Beating Test Anxiety

Working on the mental side of test anxiety can be more challenging, but as with the physical side, there are clear steps you can take to overcome it. As mentioned earlier, test anxiety often stems from lack of preparation, so the obvious solution is to prepare for the test. Effective studying may be the most important weapon you have for beating test anxiety, but you can and should employ several other mental tools to combat fear.

First, boost your confidence by reminding yourself of past success—tests or projects that you aced. If you're putting as much effort into preparing for this test as you did for those, there's no reason you should expect to fail here. Work hard to prepare; then trust your preparation.

Second, surround yourself with encouraging people. It can be helpful to find a study group, but be sure that the people you're around will encourage a positive attitude. If you spend time with others who are anxious or cynical, this will only contribute to your own anxiety. Look for others who are motivated to study hard from a desire to succeed, not from a fear of failure.

Third, reward yourself. A test is physically and mentally tiring, even without anxiety, and it can be helpful to have something to look forward to. Plan an activity following the test, regardless of the outcome, such as going to a movie or getting ice cream.

When you are taking the test, if you find yourself beginning to feel anxious, remind yourself that you know the material. Visualize successfully completing the test. Then take a few deep, relaxing breaths and return to it. Work through the questions carefully but with confidence, knowing that you are capable of succeeding.

Developing a healthy mental approach to test taking will also aid in other areas of life. Test anxiety affects more than just the actual test—it can be damaging to your mental health and even contribute to depression. It's important to beat test anxiety before it becomes a problem for more than testing.

Study Strategy

Being prepared for the test is necessary to combat anxiety, but what does being prepared look like? You may study for hours on end and still not feel prepared. What you need is a strategy for test prep. The next few pages outline our recommended steps to help you plan out and conquer the challenge of preparation.

Step 1: Scope Out the Test

Learn everything you can about the format (multiple choice, essay, etc.) and what will be on the test. Gather any study materials, course outlines, or sample exams that may be available. Not only will this help you to prepare, but knowing what to expect can help to alleviate test anxiety.

Step 2: Map Out the Material

Look through the textbook or study guide and make note of how many chapters or sections it has. Then divide these over the time you have. For example, if a book has 15 chapters and you have five days to study, you need to cover three chapters each day. Even better, if you have the time, leave an extra day at the end for overall review after you have gone through the material in depth.

If time is limited, you may need to prioritize the material. Look through it and make note of which sections you think you already have a good grasp on, and which need review. While you are studying, skim quickly through the familiar sections and take more time on the challenging parts.

Write out your plan so you don't get lost as you go. Having a written plan also helps you feel more in control of the study, so anxiety is less likely to arise from feeling overwhelmed at the amount to cover.

Step 3: Gather Your Tools

Decide what study method works best for you. Do you prefer to highlight in the book as you study and then go back over the highlighted portions? Or do you type out notes of the important information? Or is it helpful to make flashcards that you can carry with you? Assemble the pens, index cards, highlighters, post-it notes, and any other materials you may need so you won't be distracted by getting up to find things while you study.

If you're having a hard time retaining the information or organizing your notes, experiment with different methods. For example, try color-coding by subject with colored pens, highlighters, or post-it notes. If you learn better by hearing, try recording yourself reading your notes so you can listen while in the car, working out, or simply sitting at your desk. Ask a friend to quiz you from your flashcards, or try teaching someone the material to solidify it in your mind.

Step 4: Create Your Environment

It's important to avoid distractions while you study. This includes both the obvious distractions like visitors and the subtle distractions like an uncomfortable chair (or a too-comfortable couch that makes you want to fall asleep). Set up the best study environment possible: good lighting and a comfortable work area. If background music helps you focus, you may want to turn it on, but otherwise keep the room quiet. If you are using a computer to take notes, be sure you don't have any other windows open, especially applications like social media, games, or anything else that could distract you. Silence your phone and turn off notifications. Be sure to keep water close by so you stay hydrated while you study (but avoid unhealthy drinks and snacks).

Also, take into account the best time of day to study. Are you freshest first thing in the morning? Try to set aside some time then to work through the material. Is your mind clearer in the afternoon or evening? Schedule your study session then. Another method is to study at the same time of day that you will take the test, so that your brain gets used to working on the material at that time and will be ready to focus at test time.

Step 5: Study!

Once you have done all the study preparation, it's time to settle into the actual studying. Sit down, take a few moments to settle your mind so you can focus, and begin to follow your study plan. Don't give in to distractions or let yourself procrastinate. This is your time to prepare so you'll be ready to fearlessly approach the test. Make the most of the time and stay focused.

Of course, you don't want to burn out. If you study too long you may find that you're not retaining the information very well. Take regular study breaks. For example, taking five minutes out of every hour to walk briskly, breathing deeply and swinging your arms, can help your mind stay fresh.

As you get to the end of each chapter or section, it's a good idea to do a quick review. Remind yourself of what you learned and work on any difficult parts. When you feel that you've mastered the material, move on to the next part. At the end of your study session, briefly skim through your notes again.

But while review is helpful, cramming last minute is NOT. If at all possible, work ahead so that you won't need to fit all your study into the last day. Cramming overloads your brain with more information than it can process and retain, and your tired mind may struggle to recall even previously learned information when it is overwhelmed with last-minute study. Also, the urgent nature of cramming and the stress placed on your brain contribute to anxiety. You'll be more likely to go to the test feeling unprepared and having trouble thinking clearly.

So don't cram, and don't stay up late before the test, even just to review your notes at a leisurely pace. Your brain needs rest more than it needs to go over the information again. In fact, plan to finish your studies by noon or early afternoon the day before the test. Give your brain the rest of the day to relax or focus on other things, and get a good night's sleep. Then you will be fresh for the test and better able to recall what you've studied.

Step 6: Take a Practice Test

Many courses offer sample tests, either online or in the study materials. This is an excellent resource to check whether you have mastered the material, as well as to prepare for the test format and environment.

Check the test format ahead of time: the number of questions, the type (multiple choice, free response, etc.), and the time limit. Then create a plan for working through them. For example, if you have 30 minutes to take a 60-question test, your limit is 30 seconds per question. Spend less time on the questions you know well so that you can take more time on the difficult ones.

If you have time to take several practice tests, take the first one open book, with no time limit. Work through the questions at your own pace and make sure you fully understand them. Gradually work up to taking a test under test conditions: sit at a desk with all study materials put away and set a timer. Pace yourself to make sure you finish the test with time to spare and go back to check your answers if you have time.

After each test, check your answers. On the questions you missed, be sure you understand why you missed them. Did you misread the question (tests can use tricky wording)? Did you forget the information? Or was it something you hadn't learned? Go back and study any shaky areas that the practice tests reveal.

Taking these tests not only helps with your grade, but also aids in combating test anxiety. If you're already used to the test conditions, you're less likely to worry about it, and working through tests until you're scoring well gives you a confidence boost. Go through the practice tests until you feel comfortable, and then you can go into the test knowing that you're ready for it.

Test Tips

On test day, you should be confident, knowing that you've prepared well and are ready to answer the questions. But aside from preparation, there are several test day strategies you can employ to maximize your performance.

First, as stated before, get a good night's sleep the night before the test (and for several nights before that, if possible). Go into the test with a fresh, alert mind rather than staying up late to study.

Try not to change too much about your normal routine on the day of the test. It's important to eat a nutritious breakfast, but if you normally don't eat breakfast at all, consider eating just a protein bar. If you're a coffee drinker, go ahead and have your normal coffee. Just make sure you time it so that the caffeine doesn't wear off right in the middle of your test. Avoid sugary beverages, and drink enough water to stay hydrated but not so much that you need a restroom break 10 minutes into the test. If your test isn't first thing in the morning, consider going for a walk or doing a light workout before the test to get your blood flowing.

Allow yourself enough time to get ready, and leave for the test with plenty of time to spare so you won't have the anxiety of scrambling to arrive in time. Another reason to be early is to select a good seat. It's helpful to sit away from doors and windows, which can be distracting. Find a good seat, get out your supplies, and settle your mind before the test begins.

When the test begins, start by going over the instructions carefully, even if you already know what to expect. Make sure you avoid any careless mistakes by following the directions.

Then begin working through the questions, pacing yourself as you've practiced. If you're not sure on an answer, don't spend too much time on it, and don't let it shake your confidence. Either skip it and come back later, or eliminate as many wrong answers as possible and guess among the remaining ones. Don't dwell on these questions as you continue—put them out of your mind and focus on what lies ahead.

Be sure to read all of the answer choices, even if you're sure the first one is the right answer. Sometimes you'll find a better one if you keep reading. But don't second-guess yourself if you do immediately know the answer. Your gut instinct is usually right. Don't let test anxiety rob you of the information you know.

If you have time at the end of the test (and if the test format allows), go back and review your answers. Be cautious about changing any, since your first instinct tends to be correct, but make sure you didn't misread any of the questions or accidentally mark the wrong answer choice. Look over any you skipped and make an educated guess.

At the end, leave the test feeling confident. You've done your best, so don't waste time worrying about your performance or wishing you could change anything. Instead, celebrate the successful completion of this test. And finally, use this test to learn how to deal with anxiety even better next time.

Review Video: Test Anxiety
Visit mometrix.com/academy and enter code: 100340

Important Qualification

Not all anxiety is created equal. If your test anxiety is causing major issues in your life beyond the classroom or testing center, or if you are experiencing troubling physical symptoms related to your anxiety, it may be a sign of a serious physiological or psychological condition. If this sounds like your situation, we strongly encourage you to seek professional help.

Online Resources

Due to our efforts to try to keep this book to a manageable length, we've created a link that will give you access to all of your online resources:

mometrix.com/resources719/nycbritunoff

It's Your Moment, Let's Celebrate It!

Share your story @mometrixtestpreparation